THIS WON'T HELP YOU

by Craig Rypstat

Illustrations by Bill Johnson

Honey Creek Publishing, Inc.

ISBN 096544362-0

Published by Honey Creek Publishing
P.O. Box 265, North Lake, Wisconsin 53064

Books in Print

Categories: 1. Relationships, 2. Men and Women,
3. Psychology, 4. SelfHelp, 5. Case Studies, 6. Interpersonal Relationships, 7. SelfActualization, 8. Humor

TM
HONEY CREEK PUBLISHING, INC.
P.O. Box 265
North Lake, WI   53064
414.695.8815
honeycreek@aol.com

DEAR YVONNE,

YOUR SECRETS ARE SAFE WITH ME.

Love,

Craig Rypstat
9/29/98

There are a lot of people that have inspired material in this book. For instance, my friend Ron and his family collected, and I assume collect to this day, porcelain Elvis statuettes. Me and my friends, The Amorphous Super Gang, were never sure what to call the collection so we dubbed them the Elvi. It was pretty strange walking into his house and seeing glass cases filled with The King, not to mention the walls of the pool room lined from floor to ceiling with various other porcelain statuettes. We always had to stand guard over the collection while shooting pool lest a ball fly off the table and destroy one of the precious porcelain figurines. We spent a lot of time mocking the collection and the usual rebuttal was that the collection was worth a lot of money. Personally, I would have invested my money in something less tacky and more durable; like black light paintings of dogs playing poker.

As strange or humorous as the Elvi might seem, they are on par with many other belief structures I've run across. Even using a phrase like belief structure is pretty funny in and of itself. And to attach a whole paradigm and healing modality to the phrase and then charge people to help people change it, well, all I can say is caveat emptor. Let the fool and the horse he, or she, rode in on be aware that they may be on the wrong end of a colostomy bag. Or something like that.

This book is dedicated to everyone who has inspired me to laugh because of what I see as their tragically serious view of life. Yes, some of these tragically serious views were mine. I wish I could remember who said it, but "those who have lost the ability to laugh at themselves must have other people do it for them."

Foreward...

This will be brief. I hate forewards that are
longer than most chapters in the book. First
of all, read the book from front to back and
the best way to understand the writing is to
start in the upper left hand corner of the
page and then "scan" across the line of text
until it ends. Then move to the next lower
line. When you reach the bottom of the
page, start at the top of the next page. You
may have to "turn" the page. This should
help you go foreword through the book.

Introduction...

This project began because of a Bloom County cartoon. It was an earlier strip where Opus calls the Phil Donahue show and speaks passionately about penguin lust, "Peguin lust is not 'immoral and wicked.' And anybody who thinks so is just an old prude ... It's beautiful! And natural! And I for one fully support penguin lust!" When he's done Phil informs him that the topic is nun beating. Opus responds "Good Lord man ... I can't support that." So I made an affirmation out of it. Hopefully it is as funny as the strip.

From the humble beginning of wanting to help people curb their nun beating habits a full blown affirmation book grew. Well, not exactly affirmations. By the third or fourth affirmation I was bored with the style and started "ad libbing." So all the goofy ideas that usually bounced inside my head were herded, clubbed with a sledge hammer and then sent through an abattoir to be processed into vignettes, observations and an occasional affirmation. Enjoy.

Today...
I Shall Refrain
From Beating Nuns

In this hectic, stressful world sometimes it is easy to vent frustration on nuns. They seem to present themselves at the most inopportune moments and ask silly questions like "How may I help you?" What recourse is there but to beat the offending holy woman with a bat? Contrary to popular television, there are many options besides a brutal beating available.

Why not count to ten, taking a deep breath with each number? Or simply decline the invitation with a courteous "Drop dead, penguin." My personal favorite is to get into my car and run over her foot. There are many, many less violent options available.

Take a minute now and repeat the following ancient Sanskrit mantra. "Om Namaha I will not beat nuns." Repeat this verse five to ten times or until you feel free and light, with no hostility towards nuns.

Today...
I Will Check
My Duct Tape Supply

How many times have you been in need of duct tape and not had any? It is a recurring problem in my life and today I will check my supply. As I think about this important task in my co–dependent recovery, the many useful things duct tape can do come to mind. Perhaps, you too, can think of several uses. Use the following meditation to help you in this vital process.

Close your eyes and take five connected breaths. With each inhale say to yourself, "I am relaxed." Release the tension of the day. With each exhale say to yourself "What are the important uses of duct tape." When the breaths are finished see yourself using duct tape; perhaps it's green, maybe it's blue or simply gray. Feel the weight of the tape in your hands, the strength of the adhesive as you pull a piece, that is just the right length, free. See those rusty mufflers being deftly repaired, old jackets being patched, electrical wiring insulated well; whatever comes to you is right for you. It is perfect. When you are ready return to the here and now with the thought "Today I will check my duct tape supply."

I Like Flossing

Flossing our teeth, especially when done with dental floss, is a good thing. Of course we all have these voices that say flossing is a bad thing. But if we are careful enough we will find that those voices are founded in traumatic childhood events. How many vicious childhood dental floss incidents were you involved in? I can't even begin to count. How many of us dreaded the words "That's enough. Time for the dental floss." I know I did, but that doesn't mean flossing is a bad thing. It is a good thing.

To combat those negative images and voices, let's take time to think about all the good that comes from flossing. Imagine the thin string, whether you choose waxed or unwaxed you are using the perfect dental floss for you. Feel the gentle movement up and down on your teeth. Wonder at how quickly and efficiently you clean the only true evil in the world, plaque, off of your beautiful teeth. See yourself smiling confidently, knowing your flossing cleared away any unsightly food particles. Imagine how the world feels with flossed teeth. I bet it feels good.

With these thoughts, begin to see flossing as a gentle friend instead of a demonic childhood enemy. As time goes on your dreams of being chased by Frankenstein carrying a large spool of dental floss will fade. Your fear of dentistry will evaporate like the morning mist, melted by your warm, plaque–free smile. Flossing is a good thing!!

Today...
I Ponder The Universe

What a grand thing the universe is. Filled with stars and planets and black holes and all kinds of other things. It is a wonderful place and we should ponder it. Now I know that sometimes it is easy to lose sight of the importance of a pulsar during the moment, but let us take a moment to think about our big home.

And do I mean big. Take the biggest thing you can think of. Now double its size. Now double it again. If you compare that, the biggest thing you can think of multiplied by four, to the universe it is still tiny. That's how big the universe is. Wow! That is big!

To better appreciate the universe here is a meditation. Picture yourself where you are now. Okay, picture yourself pulling away from the ground. Rising up you are able to see for five miles in every direction, now ten, now one–hundred; the world finally becomes visible as a really, really big blue marble. But you keep going and the Earth pulls away. As you look towards the sun you can see Earth, Venus and that one that's closest to the sun is lost in the glare. It is still a marvelous sight. But you keep moving towards the edge of the solar system, past Mars and Saturn, then Jupiter and then the one named after some mythological water god. I think you better come back now. I'd hate for anyone to get lost with this meditation.

I Waste Time Figuring Out Lyrics

These rock musician types make stupid lyrics to their songs and we are forced to try and understand them. Like Coo, Coo, ca choo. Just what the hell does that mean? What were Paul McCartney and John Lennon thinking when they put this song together? I don't know and I have spent too much time trying to figure it out. Is coo, coo, ca choo simply a filler? Perhaps if it is run backwards it says something like "John is a dweeb." I don't know. What about the lyrics to R.E.M.'s It's The End Of The World As We Know It (and I feel fine)? Why do they feel fine? The world is ending. And just what does Lenny Bruce have to do with the world ending? And why did I spend several hours with a friend trying to understand some quietly spoken lyrics in the background of a Yes song?

You can probably think of many such songs that have difficult to grasp lyrics. Take a moment now and breath deeply. With each inhale say "I am at peace and relaxed." With each exhale ask yourself "Just what does that lyric mean" and think of a lyric you wish to understand. When you feel completely relaxed and can hear the lyric then visualize what that lyric might mean. Perhaps there is a double meaning. Maybe it's a metaphor or related symbolically to something deeply meaningful. When you have either figured out the lyric or wasted enough time return to normal consciousness. Coo coo ca choo.

Today...
I Will Use Toilet Paper

Toilet paper really is a modern miracle and I suspect most people don't use it often enough. I know I don't. It's just that toilet paper is made from trees and I have a hard time, with the state of the environment, justifying using a product which is a deforestation factor. Of course, I have a hard time justifying buying thirty to fifty pairs of underwear a month. But enough of my personal hygiene.

So as you go through your daily bowel movements, and however many you have is perfect for you, look upon toilet paper as a helpful friend, not an environmental pestilence. In many ways it is an environmental savior. Imagine how many natural resources are required to make a pair of underwear versus a roll of toilet paper. Obviously, from an environmental standpoint, toilet paper is the superior choice.

You can now boldly wipe your ass knowing you are helping the environment and maintaining good personal grooming habits. You may then proudly tell your friends "Today I used toilet paper."

Today...
I Will Hate Unconditionally

Unconditional love. Big deal. Let's face it, the world is filled with hate. Some religions seem to foster hating different religions and cultures. The political extremes seem to hate each other and choose issues that are labeled "evil" or "politically incorrect"; depending on the flavor of political psycho. People of different colors sometimes decide to hate other people of different color. It is all rather silly.

Let us cut to the chase and hate unconditionally. Let your eyes move around the room and feel hate rising from deep within your being. Move from object to object. Now begin thinking about all the people you know and allow yourself to hate them one by one. Just let it out. Pretend you are a skin head spewing racial superiority. Open your belief system to the religious right and let yourself hate tax increases and anyone who doesn't believe in God, Jesus and the Holy Trinity. Now switch to the political left and let yourself hate the religious right, tax cuts and anyone who uses phrases like "bald instead of follicly challenged." Now come back to normal.

Today I will hate unconditionally.

Today...
I Will Not Anthropomorphize
My Genitals

Enough said.

Today...
I Will Look At The World
Through The Eyes
Of A Five-Year Old

Of course I don't mean that literally. It would be horrible to blind some poor five–year old because of an affirmation. Personally I'd have to have a much better reason. What I'm talking about is figuratively using those eyes. Or more to the point, looking at everybody in the world and imagining them to be five years old.

I use this technique very often when I'm trying to figure out why some people do such silly things. Take congress for example. When I try to think of reasons why there is so much conflict, back–biting and shady dealings happening in congress it doesn't make sense to my mostly adult brain. But when I imagine our representatives being five years old suddenly things come into focus. They are all throwing temper tantrums, forming secret clubs with special passwords and holding their breaths until they get their way – this is usually called a filibuster. Actually I would like to see a congressman or congresswomen threaten to hold their breaths in a speech.

So as you go through life and the actions of people don't make sense to you, imagine them at different ages until you find the one that fits. It works for me.

I Complain

Complaining is an art that is derided too often. A good complain can make me feel better about myself, especially when someone sympathizes with my plight.

For instance, my car isn't working well. My tape deck chewed on a tape and as I went to eject the tape my interior lights went out and the deck died. It wouldn't have been that bad except I was doing 65 on the highway. After a few frantic minutes I determined the headlights were still working. Since that little incident I have discovered my running lights no longer work. So I'm stuck with a vehicle I really shouldn't drive at night, it's too cold to work outside on the wiring and I really need to replace my car anyway.

What a complaint. Do you sympathize? Even if you don't I feel better for having complained. Somehow sharing my misery makes it less. So for today... I complain.

Today...
I Will Set Goals

A man tonight told me that one of the beefs he had with younger people was that they didn't have dreams. I was buying a set of compact discs containing all of Beethoven's piano sonatas when we fell into this conversation. With that in mind I will set a goal in the solid granite of an affirmation: I will memorize all thirty–two of Beethoven's piano sonatas. Not only that, I'll learn how to play them too.

Of course this won't happen all at once, it will require practice and patience. Unless of course there is divine intervention and the notes are burned into my being. I'll bet on hard work. This leads to an important concept about dreaming, that is goals.

So many times in the course of having a dream, intermediary steps are overlooked steps. In my experience most dreams appear as a finished project. I usually get deterred from the dream by unseen hurdles. The vision remains, unfortunately the action stops. Here is a meditation to help in setting goals and maintaining the vision.

Find a quiet relaxed place and put on your favorite Beethoven sonata. With every inhale say, to yourself, "I am relaxed." With every exhale say, again to yourself, "I will set reasonable goals towards my dream." As you become more and more relaxed let your internal vision go to a dream of yours. If you don't have a dream, look for one. Now assuming you have one, or found one – a dream that is, see what you can do to foster that dream. Let your mind wander, looking for a simple action. Wait. Wait. Float. Wait. THERE IT IS! DON'T LET IT GET AWAY!. Find your internal club and strike the action, quickly. Okay now drag it into the light. Breath. Once you are sure you won't forget it come back to your waking reality.

Today...
I Strive To Remember
My Dreams

Sometimes I have dreams and don't remember them. Sometimes I have dreams, remember them and don't write them down. And sometimes I have dreams, remember them and then write them down when I wake up. That is what this affirmation is about, remembering dreams and writing them down.

Dreams are very important. As Henreid Zimmerbachs, Freud's gardener, said, "People pay Doctor Freud a lot of money to receive stupid advice about their dreams. They're the ones who are dreaming the damn things, why would he know better?" Well said, but unfortunately Henreid died in poverty. He was fired by Dr. Freud after Dr. Freud heard the above statement.

Henreid, however, had his point. You are your own best interpreter of your dreams, but I think it is necessary to keep a record of them over a long period of time. So here are pieces of advice on remember dreams and writing them down.

First, have paper and pencil, or pen if you prefer pen, near your bed. Second, repeat this mantra before you go to sleep. "Tonight as I sleep I will remember my dreams and when I awake I'll write them down before they fade away." Third, no excuses for not writing down the dreams, no whining. I know it's easy to be distracted by petty things like being late for work or the room burning around you. But don't give into temptation and flee the fire and smoke for fresh air and safety, write down your dream and then flee with your dream journal and as many porcelain Elvis figurines as you can carry. Fourth, as your dream journal accumulates entries start looking for patterns and see what they might be telling you.

Today I will strive to remember my dreams, and Henreid Zimmerbachs.

Today...
I Will Hog–tie
My Inner Child

T he little bastard has run amok. "I want an ice cream cone." "Are we there yet?" Constantly badgering me to go have fun, play and ignore the important work I need to do. So I'm going to tie up the son of a bitch and put a gag in his mouth. If you have a similar problem follow along.

Find an uncomfortable place to sit. Close your eyes and with each inhale say "I'm going to get you, you little bastard." With each exhale say "Stop that crying, or I'll give you something to cry about." When you feel you're in the proper mood start roaming the metaphorical house of your mind. Look in the closets, peer under the beds and all the secret hiding places you knew as a kid. Remember, inner children by definition are small. Once you've located the sniveling, whining shit, take out your rope and bind the hands and feet. Finally use your handkerchief as a gag. Now walk away free to pursue important matters of life secure in the knowledge that your inner child is hog–tied and gagged.

Today...
I Will Focus

Sometimes focus can be a problem. It's like you want to do something, but something else always gets in the way. Suppose you're trying to write out daily affirmations and suddenly you find yourself playing the piano. That's an example of a lack of focus. What we all need is either more focus or less distraction. Since anything can be a distraction more focus is the key.

So repeat to yourself ten times, "Today... I Will Focus." Keep the capital letters, they are for emphasis. Now a good test is if you can say all ten and keep count at the same time. Other things you can do to improve your focus is to look at a candle, a burning candle. Specifically the flame. I suppose you could use a blow torch or a stove burner, but candles are much cooler and much quieter than a blow torch. I'd find the loud, hissing sound of a blow torch distracting.

You know, there are a lot of loud noises I find distracting. There is a train that runs by my house every night about midnight. Oh sometimes it arrives around quarter til, sometimes near quarter after. I haven't noticed it arrive any later than half past midnight. Anyway, it makes a loud squeaking sound and blows a loud air horn. I find that very distracting and it usually derails my train of thought. I might have to move so I don't get distracted by it.

So, Today... I Will Focus. I'll recognize those things that distract me and take steps to reduce how much they affect my life and use the simple tools listed above to improve my ability to focus.

I Honor
My Inner Tyrant

Too often tyrants are misunderstood. Napoleon was simply trying to collect Europe's great art treasures. Hitler wanted a good soccer team. And Saddam Husein wants to be understood. They just go to extremes in their temper tantrums. We all have our own "Innter Tyrants" and I have a special meditation to honor that important part of the psyche..

Find a place where you feel like you're completely in control. Get tense and with every inhale say 'I can do it all. I'm that good.' With every exhale say 'There's nothing wrong with being a swaggering, overbearing, tinplated dictator with delusions of godhood.' When you feel wonderfully tyrannical find the inner throne room and grandly cross the floor to your raised dais. You climb to your throne and regally sit. Thrill as you pass judgment on everyone, knowing you have complete mastery. Notice your subjects as they view you with awe, respect and fear. Dispense justice on your lowly charges until you are ready to return. Slowly let your tyranny fade, knowing you can be a tyrant whenever you like.

Today...
I Steal
My Grandmother's Walker

Grandmothers can be a real pain in the ass. "Change the channel for me, dear." "Would you be so kind as to get me a glass of water." "I need a fresh collostomy bag." Nag, nag, nag, nag, nag, nag. And they follow you around too. My grandma followed me around the house for three hours yesterday. All she said was "I'm having chest pains. Will you please take me to the hospital." Bitch. I eventually took her and the doctors determined the pain was being caused by her wearing my little sister's training bra.

I've lost it. Grandma's in the living room napping. All day long she's been complaining about the television, "Where's Bob Barker? Where's Bob Barker?" I've had to listen to that all day as she's thumped behind me in her walker. I can't stand it anymore. I've got to sneak in and take her only means of transportation. Today I Will Steal My Grandmother's Walker.

I Shit On Myself

I admit it, I have a lot of problems in my life. I use to deny my responsibility for them, but after years of reading self–help books and watching talk shows I now own my own problems. So I must be a pretty lousy human being for having fucked–up my life so badly. I know this is "negative thinking" and I shouldn't do that, but I don't care. I usually feel better after I've given those negative voices in my head room to roam.

For example: 'You idiot, why in the hell are you writing an affirmation like this? Nobody's going to want to read it, let alone do the idiotic meditation you have planned. Where did you ever come up with such a lame idea. You know what I think you should do? Well I'll tell you. I think you should sell those ugly Elvis statuettes, get a haircut and finish that associates degree. You've been bitching about your life for so long you've forgotten how to have one. You're worthless and weak and ...'

Okay, I think that's about enough. Time to put the brakes on Mr. Negativity. "Mr. Negativity I want you to be quiet now, thank you for your opinions". Go fuck yourself, pencil neck. Now for those who want to do this meditation find a place where you can relax. You can't shut me away, I own you. Now breath deeply and relax, remembering all the tensions of the day and the voices associated with them. When they are all clamoring for attention pick the loudest one and think with a firm internal voice, "you moron what does that mean?" Say, "You may speak to me now." Let the voice speak, listen to all it has to say and then firmly think "Kindly be quiet and thank you for your opinions." Write down what the voice said, this will allow you to learn about it and be better able to cope. For as Lao Tsu said "Know your enemy as you know yourself." That's Sun Tsu, geek. And I control the supply lines.

20

I Live Boldly

L ife is to be lived boldly. Take risks, take big risks. Put yourself in the spotlight and then dance. And dance boldly. Because, as they said in Strictly Ballroom, "A life lived in fear is a life half lived."

As I think about it I probably live about an eighth of my life. When I wake up in the morning I'm afraid my radio is playing too loud and turn it down so I don't bother my neighbors. At work I don't say anything people might find offensive, I talk about the weather and 60 Minutes. When I come home at night I do boldly water my plants. Nobody better get in my way when I've a mind to water plants or else they'll leave with a pair of soggy shoes.

Who am I kidding? There is no way to boldly water plants. About the only thing in my life that could be considered bold is this affirmation book. I keep wondering if people will think I'm weird. You know all the references to Elvis, the meditations and my habit of giggling uncontrollably at the phrase 'feather duster.'

But I will write this book boldly. However, if anyone is offended by any of the writing I am deeply, deeply sorry and beg your forgiveness. Please forgive me, if you write me a letter, I'll never write an affirmation like the one that offended you again. I'm so ashamed.

21

I Am Happy

I am happy because somewhere the worst sex is happening right now and I'm not a part of it. ... Hey wait. Somewhere the best sex is happening right now and I'm not a part of that either. Aw, now I'm depressed.

I Am A Victim

L ife is about being a victim. Period. The Universe hates us all and only rewards those who complain the loudest. Why? Because that's the way it is. I'm a victim, you're a victim, wouldn't you like to be a victim too? It's easy. Just say to yourself "I'm a victim. I'm a victim. I'm a victim."

It works every time for me. Whenever I use this magic phrase I'm reminded of how shitty my life is. And I know it's not my fault. God made me this way because God hates me. That's all there is to it. And I know God hates you too. Just because.

Here is a victim's meditation. Find a place where you feel insecure, broken and alone. Breath in and feel the air oppressing you. Yeah, that's right, oppressing you with sixteen pounds per square inch. Every step you take is mired in this so called "life giving" air. And who cares you? NOBODY!! Now with each exhale feel how trapped you are in your body, how much pain it causes you. Never being able to run through a door and leave a silhouette. It's all a cruel joke. Now when you feel completely victimized understand that this is your natural state. The state of victimhood.

Have a cruddy day. You deserve it.

I Am A Mountain

I am a mountain. Large, majestic, beautiful, full of life. I am a mountain. My roots go into the earth and my crown pierces the sky. I am a mountain. I hold secrets and dreams unseen by mortals. I am a mountain. I breathe the life of the planet. I shelter the animals. I am ever present and magical. I am a mountain.

You are also a mountain. Take in a breath and own your majesty. Own your power. Own that your trees have been clear cut. Own that a ski hill is being developed. Hey. It might suck to be a mountain. Imagine never being able to move. That would really suck. Think about miners poking around looking for stuff. Forest fires and earthquakes would suck. What about erosion? What about hunters? What about airplanes crashing into you?

Being a mountain would suck.

You Are Powerful

You are a powerful human being. You live your life with authenticity. Everybody loves you. You are beautiful and kind and children run to you. Wild animals come to your call.

Yeah, like I know. I'm writing this from an apartment in Madison, Wisconsin. I've never met you and I'm just making this shit up so that you'll like this affirmation. I don't believe a word of what I wrote in the last paragraph. I'm just appealing to your vanity and it worked. You read this affirmation. I hope you bought this so I can receive royalties for your neediness.

You are completely pathetic. Buying a book written by a complete stranger intended to pander to your weak, little ego. You codependent narcissistic fuck, get a life.

I'm No Longer Pathetic

It is official. I am no longer pathetic. How do I know? Well apart from the certificate mailed to me by the "I'm No Longer Pathetic Society" there is the overwhelming willingness to not call people who don't call me back.

Let me explain. For a very long time, perhaps my entire natural life where I could intelligently use a telephone, I had the unusual habit of believing people when they said they'd call me back. Call me stupid, but I believed them. I wanted so badly to believe them that when they didn't call I'd make up excuses for them.

"Maybe they forgot."

"I must have said something to offend them in our last conversation. I better call and apologize."

"Something awful has happened to them. I bet they're trapped under a bus at this very moment, wishing they were talking to me on the telephone. Oh my God, I better call and make sure they're okay."

There were infinite variations and they all concluded with me calling. I was a complete schmuck. Now many of these calls were made in the hopes of possibly getting laid. Perhaps a lot can be forgiven for that end, so to speak, but not anymore. I demand integrity. I demand people call me when they say they will. I demand to interpret someone who doesn't call me when they say they will as a sign they are evil incarnate. I know they are and I'm better off with them out of my life. Of course, my phone hasn't rung in weeks. Better than being pathetic.

I Have Achieved
Messlibrium

Messlibrium, that ancient concept so difficult to grasp, has finally been achieved. Sure, in quantum mechanics messbilrium is easy to visualize; all those atoms spinning around, never standing still. This led to Max Planc to remark, "the atom shall always be a mess." But in the macroscopic the concept that Mess can neither be created nor destroyed boggled my mind for a while.

Einstein had some insights between Mess and energy, the famous Mess = Energy multiplied by the size of the room cubed (M = ER3), and I finally understand how Messlibrium works in my life. I've decided to clean up my apartment and as it becomes more clean my office became more messy. It finally dawned on me that I may be experiencing this phenomenon.

To test the theories I measured the mass of the mess in my apartment and office over a three day period and, surprise, the mess remained constant. So I have to have 54.5 Jm3 of mess in my life. This is such a relief to know that science has finally validated the clutter of my life.

Today...
I Hang Out
Unconditionally

How often do you place conditions on your hanging out? If you're like me, probably far too often. When I'm done balancing my checkbook then I'll hang out. Once I have finished the big project at work I'll have time to hang out. After I've gotten married, raised a family and retired there will be time to hang out properly.

Enough! We must take the time to hang. It is important to find just that right spot, away from everything else, and just ... hang. Relax. Watch the world go by. Simply not worry about things. It's not that difficult and I have a meditation that will help you hang out.

Close your eyes. With each inhale think "I am relaxed." With each exhale think "I am hanging out, this is nice." When you are relaxed and hangin' go to your favorite hang–out spot. See yourself finding your favorite chair and sitting in your favorite spot, maybe you even have a beverage. Now hang. Just hang. When you've had enough return slowly.

Now get back to work. You've wasted enough time already.

I Am Proud
Of My Big Nose

How often have you been taunted, passed over for promotion and imprisoned for having a big nose? Like me, you have probably lost count, but yet don't know where to turn to combat the nose discrimination rampant in our society.

I am so sick of the blatant noseism that happens to me everyday. "You can't have a loan Mr. Rypstat because your nose is too big." "You aren't licensed to be transporting that big a nose in that small a vehicle, you'll have to get into the squad car." "Hey, are those your nostrils or two black holes?" This from a waiter to a small nosed person at a restaurant, "Forget the bill, I'll just give it to the guy with the huge schnazz. He deserves it."

Well, to quote a great movie, "I'm mad as hell and I'm not going to take it anymore." And I invite you to join me. Never again will I stifle a sneeze for fear of blowing someone against a wall. Never again will I hide my admiration of W.C. Fields and Jimmy Durante. Never again will I tolerate the jibes of cruel and mean spirited small nosed people. I will blow my nose whenever I want. I will braid my nose hair if I want to. I will not tolerate those who treat me as nasally inferior, they're the ones with the small sinus passages.

Join me, my brother and sister big noses. Our kind are every where; of every race, creed and religion. Help me establish nose–equity for all.

I Am Mature

There are certain rites of passage in our culture that are milestones on the way to maturity. Potty training, driving, graduation from high school and learning to program the VCR are only a few examples. The other night I reached a maturation point I'd never imagined.

I was in the bathroom after brushing my teeth when I noticed the toilet paper roll was empty. With only a moments hesitation I changed a fresh roll into the holder. At the time I was thinking it would be better than sitting on the toilet and realizing the paper was gone. This leads inevitably to the awkward "my ass hasn't been wiped" walk to where the paper is stored and then the pants about the ankles shuffle back to the toilet. I decided to avoid the whole ritual. And somewhere an angel got their wings.

31

I Respect Boundaries

Boundaries come in all shapes and sizes. There are physical boundaries like prison bars, intellectual boundaries such as those used in evil calculus equations, emotional boundaries which stop us from throttling assholes who cut us off in traffic and spiritual boundaries which prevent us from truly knowing how to use Woolite effectively. All of these different types of boundaries need to be recognized, understood and respected according to their merits.

How many times has someone set a boundary that made no sense. For example, a friend of mine was told at age three that he shouldn't play with matches. He rightfully ignored that dictum and accidentally burned down the house. Luckily no one was injured and he learned by experience, not blind rule observance, not to play with matches. I'm sure it is a lesson that he has not forgotten.

So maybe today's affirmation should read:

I Respect Those Boundaries That Deserve To Be Respected

I think Henry David Thoreau was completely correct when he wrote On The Duty of Civil Disobedience. We have an obligation to ourselves to question and weigh those rules, boundaries, which are thrust upon us by society. Why can't I have my own Napalm? What's the harm in destroying government data bases? And who said bathing was a necessary social function? These are all questions that can only be answered upon deeper contemplation of one's own moral and ethical standards. So,

I Question Every Boundary I Encounter...

I Leave My Emotional Body Closed

on't do it. Just don't do it. Do not, under any circumstances, activate your emotional body because if you do you are completely screwed. Imagine a life where every–fucking–thing is an issue. Getting up in the morning, talking with people, even going out to dinner will push buttons, bring up issues and generally make your life a living emotional hell.

The more "enlightened" I become the more I realize how much easier life was when I was in denial. I got so much done. I didn't worry about how my actions affected other people. I blissfully, or at least very numbly, went about my life. That ended the moment I started feeling. I've tried everything to stop feeling; drugs alcohol, Gilligan's Island reruns, but I can't.

If you are feeling like you have a problem with addiction, ignore that feeling. Do more of your addictive behavior. Please believe me, the problems associated with knowing your issues far outweigh the problems associated with not knowing your issues.

I Bring The Apocalypse To Those Who Want It

The Apocalypse is coming. So say the Seventh Day Adventists and a bunch of other wacko prophets. I say we give it to them. The next time you are told the Apocalypse is coming, follow that person to their home. When they least expect it, let the Apocalypse rain down on their life. Raze their house, destroy the car and take their pets. Make their life a living hell.

This will be done as a humanitarian effort. These people who are so insistent that the Apocalypse is coming will never be happy until it does. But why should it ruin everyone else's day? Hopefully once the Apocalypse visits these people, in a very real and personal way, they will let go of their need to have their lives ruined and become happier for the experience.

I am Not
A Princess

I feel sorry for you if you were treated like little princesses while growing up. The truth is you are either a narcissistic, overbearing, demanding bitch of a woman who has never learned how to be kind, loving and giving, Or you're a narcissistic, overbearing, demanding bitch of a man who is very confused and has never learned how to be kind, loving and giving. Either way, it's high time someone helped you.

Breath deep. With each inhale say 'I am relaxed.' With each exhale say 'I am not a princess.' After five complete breaths begin to let your mind wander to the first time you felt special, unique, totally loved. See it. Hear it. Feel it. Be there. Now completely destroy that image. It no longer serves you. Repeat this until all your memories of being a special princess have faded to nothing. Return to normal consciousness fully aware of how bland, boring and identical you are.

Glad I could help.

I Take Everything Personally

For a very long time I didn't take responsibility for the messages I was communicating to people. When someone was rude to me I always thought it was their problem. I didn't do anything to cause them to behave that way towards me. I now know differently. The reaction I get from people is the message I communicated to them. The guy who cuts me off in traffic does so because I wanted him to on some level. Same with other unexpected behaviors I experience. I now take everything personally, and so should you.

Find a relaxing place where you can breath deeply and say with each inhale "I am relaxed" and with each exhale say "It's all personal." As you drift into deeper accountability for your communication realize the people that cut you off while driving, they do it because they don't like you. The cashier at the grocery store who's rude doesn't like your attitude. People have bad days because you're alive. You are responsible for everybody's behavior, except your own. Everybody else is controlling you. Hey, if everybody is responsible for your behavior and you are responsible for everybody's behavior, who is really responsible? Oh no, another confusing mediation. I'm sorry, please return now feeling fully relaxed and refreshed and ready to face the day with a bright, shiny face.

I'm A Winner

Green Bay rules. They kicked San Francisco's collective ass all over what used to be Candle Stick Park. It was great, they won. They're winners. And I back the Pack, so I'm a winner too.

I'm going to buy a whole Packer wardrobe so I can be more of a winner. I'm going to get a baseball hat, 'cause nothing says 'I'm a Winner' more than a winning teams baseball hat; except a jersey. Then I'm going to buy a jersey just like Brett Farve wears. He's a winner. He's the NFL's MVP. And I'll be a winner just like him if I'm wearing a baseball hat and a genuine jersey just like Brett wears. I'm a winner.

I'm A Loser

Green Bay sucks. More specifically the refs who worked the National League Championship suck. They ignored an illegal pick play, allowed Eric Williams to use illegal hands to the face on Reggie for the entire game and made a bad defensive pass interference against the Pack. Anyway, Green Bay lost to Dallas. The Packers are losers. Wisconsin is a loser state. The Bucks are losers. The Brewers are losers. Every time I wear my official Packer–wear I'll be painting a loser sign on my body. I'm a loser.

I Order My Psyche

Between the works of Virginia Satir, John Bradshaw, Robert Bly, Michael Meade, Robert Moore, Eugene Gillette, John Grinder and Richard Bandler, just to name a few, I now know I have more parts in my psyche than I know what to do with and I'm not really sure who or what is controlling my life. Luckily, I have a meditation which really helps me sort things out.

Take several deep breaths. With each inhale say to yourself "I am relaxed." With each exhale say to yourself "I will order my psyche." When you feel relaxed, find and communicate with each of these parts : Your Sovereign, The Warrior, The Magician, The Lover, The Wounded Child, The Wounded Adult, The Hero, The Lost Child, The Abandoned Child, The Perfectionist, The Blacksheep, The Joyful Child, The Responsible One, The Narcissist, The Judge, The Jury, The Executioner, The David Bowe Fan, The Fanatic, The Cook, The Maid, The Elvis Statuette Collector, The Meditator, The Mango Madness Drinker and whatever special fragments you may have in your psyche. Make sure each one is fully contacted, fully listened to and happy. This meditation should only take five to ten years to complete.

Today...
I Reevaluate Feminism

I have gotten tired of being blamed for the world's problems. This complex comes from being a white male and growing up in a somewhat progressive household. Well I'm sick of it, so here are a couple of shots at the feminist establishment.

I define the feminist establishment as those people who are politically motivated to champion women as victims. Actually I think they are trying to legislate the status women as victims. If I was being Politically Correct I'd have inserted a "into women somewhere. If questioned about it I'd angrily reply that the q was silent."

First shot. If these people were really interested in equality they'd be lobbying for young women to be included in the selective service and any subsequent drafts. Seeing that they aren't willing to shoulder one of the burdens that comes with being male I can only assume they want to obtain "power" without paying the price.

Second shot. Why are these people so unhappy? Show me an adamant feminist and I'll show you someone who has a difficult time being happy. I can respect that their lives may be miserable, but do they have to legislate their misery and try to convince people to be as unhappy as they are? I'm tired of it. So I'm going against the hidden agenda of feminism and being happy.

Third shot. To paraphrase George Carlin, have you ever noticed that the people who are the most insistent feminists are people you wouldn't ever want to fuck. Look, I can spot an angry feminist a mile away. For women its the short black hair cut into a bob, a pear shaped body, perma–frown and two emotions: rage and anger. For men it's long unkept hair, a tooth–pick shaped body, perma–wimper sometimes covered with a beard (although that is too masculine for some male feminists) and a simpering need to be approved of by hostile, angry women.

Let's face it, part of the agenda of feminism is noble. I do believe there should be equality in economic situations. I, however, believe that power is not defined by economic clout, but rather by my power to create my own happiness. But then again I'm a white male oppressor who has bought into the hegemony and am enjoying the benefits of a national power structure directed towards people in my demographic.

Today I will reevaluate feminism.

I Believe...
In Myself

Today I will believe in myself. How many times have we allowed ourselves not to pursue things because we don't believe in ourselves. Far too often. So today whenever you feel like you don't believe in yourself just say "I Believe In Myself" and I'm sure things will work out.

I Read...
The Book of Swizen 13:23

And yeah verily did the Lord come down in a mighty vengeance. Upon his brow he wore the holy moldy cabbage and the people quailed. For they new the end was nigh.

And St. Swizen said 'Lord why dost thou wear the holy moldy cabbage? We are your most humble servants. What have we done to anger you?'

And the Lord, His voice ringing like a soprano in the Vienna Boys Choir, spoke 'Thou hast forsaken Me and in vengeance I shall spite you.'

And St. Swizen asked 'Don't you mean smite us, not spite us, oh Lord?

Sheepishly the Lord spoke, his voice like squeaking mice, 'Of course, I meant smite you. Just a test. Ha Ha Ha. And you passed. But now it's time for a smiting.'

St. Swizen spoke as the Lord raised the dreaded Yak Tail Of Doom. 'Lord, Your Inner Child is feeling abandoned and is acting out. We still love You. It's just that, well, new times call for new gods. Our casting of golden idols was nothing personal. Please come to my house and we can discuss this over non–alcoholic beer.'

And the Lord said 'You are right. Sometimes I get lost in my feelings and take them out on people who don't deserve it. A tasty non–alcoholic beer sounds good right now.'

I Want...
To Move Like Cartoons

I have tried, I have really tried, but I just can't move like those cartoon characters. Every time I run my feet always catch the ground. Even if I try to run really really fast my feet never slip and slide on the ground, unless I'm on ice. If I'm on ice and try to run like Wiley Coyote my feet do slip and then I fall on my back. Every time. It's painful and I'm getting tired of the emergency room people always laughing at me. Fuck them. I know I can move like those cartoon characters if I just work hard enough.

So far the success I've had includes eating carrots, shooting my guns so that I get lifted into the air (okay, I had to jump a little) and being able to say "Great horney toads" to where fifty percent of the time people know I'm impersonating Yosemite Sam. As great as these accomplishments are, it's not enough. I want more.

I want to be able to be blown up by dynamite and then be fine afterwards. The first time I tried that one I wound up in the hospital for three weeks. I want to be able to run through doors and leave a silhouette. All I ever do is break my nose. I want to have working air brakes on my airplane so I can stop it just above the ground like Bugs did.

I'm not asking for that much. It's simple really. I just want to move like cartoon characters.

I Shame...
Myself*

Shame yourself or maybe your brother
    Hang a guilt trip perhaps a shame ball on your mother,
    Then grab dear old Dad, baby sister too
And shame yourselves into a good case of blues,
Do it just for fun or do it out of spite
But just shame yourself throughout the night

Happy happy joy to every girl and boy
Tape a cheese log to your nose
(I really like that line so I kept it in.)
Why hang cruelties on others
when you can put them on yourself

* Sung to the tune of Ren and Stimpy

Today...
I Use Non Sequiturs

As we go through life many wonderful things happen. Metal–Oxide–Semi–Conductor transistors will freeze out below certain temperatures. That is, there will not be enough thermal energy to free the weakly bound electrons, in the case of an n–type semiconductor, to the conduction band. And though flowers may bloom in the spring of the year, they will always live in my heart for you. Red wine goes well with fish.

Oh what a many splendid thing ducks are, if only they were flightless. Morning comes but once a day, brining with it all this stuff. The telephone rang, Harold took out his snub nosed revolver expecting trouble and Lola slowly lifted the receiver from the cradle. "A feather duster, two g–strings and a case of Ping–Pong balls," said Detective Robbins. "It must have been a strange game of twister to have ended in murder."

May The Force stomp you into little pieces.

I Know...
Who Jesus Was

I've been hearing this name a lot in the past few weeks, Jesus. Who was this guy? I asked a friend who Jesus was and they told me to read the Bible. I asked what the Bible was and they just laughed. So I went to the library and tried to check one out and you know what? They had about fifteen different versions, each of them around 2000 pages. I didn't know which one was correct so I checked out the Cliff's notes version. It was still fifty pages, crammed with this incredibly tiny print.

As far as I can tell Jesus is a guy who had two crosses to bear in his life. One was being a carpenters son and the other was actually bearing a cross. Both seem pretty dreadful to me. Anyway, for having died at age thirty–three he seemed to have a big mouth. He was always talking, and all he talked about was common sense stuff. People with low self–esteem shall inherit the Earth. Big deal. Although I suppose being nailed to a cross for three days was sort of a bummer. I wonder if he preached from up there.

If nothing else I understand Hanukkah better now.

Writing Love Letters Is Fun

My Fairest Apple Pimple,

When I see you walking down the street my heart goes all bump–bump–bump, just like a car with bad suspension driving over a lot of pot holes. And it feels like my cv–joint is about to go bad. And bad in a really bad way, like it'll break and I'll have to get a new car. And that's just from seeing you walk.

And when you talk to me, I can't help but swoon. "I'll have a Big Mac, extra large fries, two apple pies and a Diet Coke to go," is music to my ears, but it's not what you say rather how you say it. Like it is something you'd say only to someone you love with your entire soul. Like the way I love you.

Sometimes you use the drive through and I love the way you use your blinkers, always courteously indicating which direction you're going to turn. You usually turn left. I sense how gently you turn the steering wheel, the love you have for all the people driving around you. Only loving, soulfull women use their blinkers.

If I only knew where you work. If I only knew your favorite color. If I only knew the right words to say. If I only knew the type of car to drive. If I only knew your name. If I only knew how to introduce myself to you I'm sure our love would out-shine the stars.

Maybe if I write this in my affirmation book someday you'll read it and know that I meant you. Then you'll come rushing into my arms with terms of love and tenderness, just like I dream about. This is shit, she'll never like me. I quit.

50

I Sympathize With People Who Have Bad Hair

Picture a small child. A small child with brown locks of hair. A small child who wants nothing more than to have his hair look good. This small child goes to the barber for several years, never a decent cut. He moves on to the salons at the tender age of ten and learns of the cruelties hidden behind the glamour of a shampoo and style. The stylists will lie. They say anything and everything to the young man to convince him his hair looks good. "It's beautiful." "Your mother is going to love it." "Stunning." All lies. Lies aimed at getting this fragile, naive and hopeful young man to buy hair care products. First it was combs, then brushes and as the young man worked his fingers raw delivering Grit magazine the amount of styling gel, conditioner and herbally balanced shampoo always increased.

He learns that it doesn't matter and tries more radical hair procedures; dreadlocks, perms, coloring, tinting, frosting, silicon scalp implants to shape the head, corn row, bee hives, buns and finally bouffant. Nothing worked. Nothing. How do I know this story so well? I was that small child.

Spirit Is...
In My Life

S pirit is a part of my life and Spirit talks to me. Well, talking isn't the right word, Spirit sort of hums. And the thing that bothers me is Its off key. When I meditate I occasionally hear this tuneless, off key humming "Hmmm hmmm hmm hhhm hmm hmm hhmmm hhmmm." It just goes on and on and on. It's really annoying.

The great spiritualists have always been able to commune with Spirit. I keep thinking I may have the potential to really tap into the Universe, but for now it's like I share my meditation space with crazy Uncle Ernie. He also hummed off tune all the time and it drove me nuts. I hope Spirit has more to offer than Uncle Ernie's tuneless humming.

I'm In L • O • V • E

I just saw the woman of my dreams in Spiritual Babes, the magazine devoted to bringing spiritually empowered chicks to the men who love them. Candy Stephenson is one deep woman. Her poetry makes me weep. It's so touching.

On Spirit's winds I am upheld
Ever aloft, ever safe, ever loved

What a babe. She's published a book of poetry, studied Egyptian mythology, worked with Mother Theresa in Calcutta for a year, is 35–25–36D, knows Sanskrit and has a great ass. She is spiritualicious.

53

Today...
I Will Find A Playmate

Hey babe, I know a lot games play we could play.

Like what? Like Chutes and Ladders, yeah you'd like that one.

What else?

Oh baby, I've got Monopoly, I've got Life, I've got Parcheesi, I've got Sorry, I've Pay Day. I've got lots games, lots of games.

Sure I've got toys too. I've got a Mr. Potato Head. He's lots of fun, takin' off his nose and legs and glasses and then putting them back on again. That's real fun. Oh yeah, oh yeah; I've got Ragedy Ann and Ragedy Andy. I've got stuffed toys. I've got GI Joe. I've even got a Six Million Dollar Man. And that's just the beginning. I've got a whole room full of toys, I've even got an Easy Bake Oven. I know you'd like that.

What do you mean 'When did the bar start letting in loonies?' Hey, if you don't want to play just tell me. I can find lots of friends who will play with me. See if I care. Cooty head.

Hey baby, you like games?

I Seek...
Attention

I am great. I am stupendous. I leap tall shrubs in a single bound. I open doors without effort. I drive my car well. I am ripped. I am cut. I am huge. I run marathons for fun. I throw fastballs at 98 miles per hour. I drive Formula One race cars. Three days ago a crushed an aluminum can with one hand. Before I walk into a room women swoon. While at parties I am the center of attention. When I leave a room the men swoon. I lead like Fred Astaire and follow like Ginger Rogers. I play the jazz Tuba and have no peer. Three weeks ago I took out the garbage. Four score and seven years ago I wasn't born. This is making no sense. I need serious professional help. I can't stop. Help me, please.

I Am Having...
My Tape Player Repaired

I only wanted to lose ten pounds. A friend said they had a great tape that helped them lose the weight they wanted to so I borrowed it and played it as I went to sleep. I didn't know my tape player was messed up. It played the damn tape backwards and now I weigh three–hundred pounds, none of my clothes fit and my apartment is littered with the remains of what must have been a huge binge.

The thing is, I don't even remember how I got this way. The tape supposedly used hypnosis and something called double induction to help people lose weight. I must have gone into a deep hypnotic trance where all I wanted to do was eat. I am so screwed. I'm going to get my tape player fixed and then play that tape forward, as soon as I find something to wear. I hope it works as well forward as it did backwards..

I Determine...
How Spiritual I Am

By taking this simple test.

Yes   *No*   *Spiritual Attainment*

☐   ☐   My bed is made everyday.

☐   ☐   I understand the metaphors of the Bible.

☐   ☐   I have had a death experience which killed the ego.

☐   ☐   I have attained enlightenment.

☐   ☐   When I have a bowel movement it smells like roses.

☐   ☐   I pay my bills on time.

☐   ☐   I have attained physical immortality.

☐   ☐   I don't drink caffeine.

☐   ☐   I have raised the dead.

☐   ☐   I own or lease at least three Elvis statuettes.

For every 'Yes' give yourself a point. For every 'No' beat yourself with a two–by–four for three minutes. You are spiritual when you achieve ten points. Good luck.

I Help...
The Fashion Impaired

There are an estimated twenty–million Americans who are fashion impaired. This debilitating disease causes them to wear plaid Bermuda shorts, speedos and bikinis without consideration for those who have to view them, hats with plastic fruit as decoration and join the Shriners. It is an insidious disease and must be addressed. We, as a nation, must not tolerate the plight of the fashionless.

If you have fashion sense reach out. Go to that person who does not accessorize well and offer your assistance. Go shopping with them, help them destroy the clothes that are twenty years out of date, even simply pointing out good fashion magazines will inspire them to greater levels of fashion awareness.

Of course there is a risk. Many people who are fashion illiterate are comfortable in their ignorance. They enjoy the stares and stifled giggles. They may react with hostility and even violence, but you must persevere. You must persevere because lives are at stake, good looking lives are at stake. It is not enough to merely survive, one must look good doing it.

Reach out today. Help today. Help create a better looking tomorrow.

I Seek...
To Understand
Athleticaholics

My name is Frank. I'm an Altheticaholic. I joined AA seven years ago and began the twelve step recovery program. It saved my life.

Seven years ago I was a raging Altheticaholic. ESPN, ESPN2, ABC Sports, CBS Sports, Monday Night Football, Softball league in the summer, bowling once a week with the guys during the winter, closets filled with useless sporting equipment. I was a textbook example of sports gone bad. And I couldn't see it. I was blind to my own self–destructive habits. It took the love and caring of my family and friends to help me see my problem.

One Sunday afternoon, between the football double–header, I was confronted. I was shooting pool in the basement, trying to perfect a shot I had seen Minnesota Fats make on ESPN2 Saturday after the Notre Dame – Purdue game. Man was that a blow–out. I'll never understand why those two teams play any-more. Notre Dame outclasses them so much. It hasn't been a contest in years. Oh. Sorry. Sometimes I slip. My wife calls to me from upstairs that she needs some help moving the couch. I run up the stairs, two at a time, and find myself surrounded by people.

My boss is there, our pastor, all my kids, my wife and my best friend Jim. "Frank," Pastor Mike begins "you've got a problem. You're an athleticaholic and you need help." Of course I denied the charge, but then they step back and show me all these boxes. There were at least ten of them, all filled with useless sports equipment; broken tennis rackets, musty baseballs, rotted gloves, flat basketballs, three bicycles, a treadmill and several pairs of skis (downhill and cross country) among others. Then everyone told me how I was obsessed with sports, citing specific examples. I was overwhelmed and when I saw, when I saw how sick I was I knew I had to change.

I was shipped to Hazelton to dry out. I went cold turkey and was placed in a sports–free isolation ward. It was hell, I'm sure most of you can imagine or have been there yourself, not knowing the scores, wondering how my favorite players and teams were doing, hoping my skills would still be sharp once the treatment was over. Luckily they gave me plenty of alcohol and valium to take the edge off. It only took three weeks for me to be declared clean. I left with a pad full of prescriptions and Mr. Boston's bartenders guide.

With the help of my sponsor and AA meetings I was able to "stay off the playing field," as we say. Of course I had a few close calls, but I'm standing here, not speaking about sports, living proof that the program works.

Now I'd like to introduce our keynote speaker, Joe Montana.

I Continue The Beatings... Until Morale Improves

C ome on you no good lay–abouts. Be happy, damn your eyes. What's wrong with all of you? In my day we were happy even though we had to dance in mine fields. In the winter. Naked. We didn't have much, but we were happy. Happy I tell you. But not you lazy, rotten, no–good, blasted scum.

Oh Oh Oh I want my MTV. Well FUCK YOU. No television for today, not even Frasier. Sure you have all these new fangled thingies; Nintendo, cellular telephones and dirt. Did we have these things when I was growing up? No, I tell you, but our morale was high. And when we were asked to march off to war did we complain? No, we picked up our muskets and went to Valley Forge, because that's what General Washington said had to be done. We trusted our leadership, not like you smelly, rotten clothes wearing, tofu eating, tai chi practicing, long haired, hippy, pinko commie British supporting Tories out there.

Watergate. Viet Nam. The S&L scandal. The ozone layer. Our government lied to us about the CIA. Gay rights. Lesbian rights. Fetal rights. Politically correct. Politically incorrect. You pathetic, no account, unmotivated, corporeal punishment disliking, composting generation Xers have so many excuses. In my day we didn't even know what the ozone layer was, let alone care that it was being depleted by our rampant use of air conditioners and herbal facial wraps. We were happy I tell you.

Well, the beatings will simply continue until morale improves. And no more clean nails in the boards for the likes of you. That's right. I'm putting the rusty nails back in and there will be no bactine to clean the wounds afterwards. Now get happy, damn you to hell and back.

I Watch...
The Emotional World News
With Dan Rather and Connie Chung

Dan...Right now I'm feeling like I'm not good enough. I've had this problem ever since I was a kid. I'd get up in front of big audiences and this voice would say 'You're not good enough Dan.' Well today I'm good enough to give the news and I'm in.

Connie...What you said really speaks to me. Sometimes I feel like I'm not good enough. Not good enough to be respected in my field and not good enough to conceive a baby. But right now I'm feeling happy. I'm in.

Dan...In a press conference today at the White House the President announced that his inner child wasn't getting out enough to play and he was therefore going to Camp David to play hide–and–go–seek, capture the flag and Marco Polo with the Joint Chiefs of Staff.

Connie...In the world of business, the stock market closed early today so that traders could go home and spend time either meditating or with their families. Many people disagreed with the closing and were quickly shamed into silence.

Dan...Today in Germany a man, Gunter Hilmich, got that he can simply change his belief system by believing something else. He promptly believed gravity didn't affect him and jumped out of a second story window, breaking both his legs.

I Take Thoreau...
Figuratively

Thoreau once said 'Perhaps we should never procure a new suit, however ragged or dirty the old, until we have so conducted, so enterprised or sailed in some way, that we feel like new men in the old, and that to retain it would be like keeping new wine in old bottles.' I, unfortunately, took this too literally and now have an old, dirty and tattered wardrobe that occasionally smells very bad.

Did Thoreau really mean that people who don't change very much shouldn't buy new clothes? Perhaps. Then again he lived alone in a dirt house for over a year, was imprisoned and had a fairly low opinion of the human race. Maybe he wasn't that sociable a character. Perhaps he used his clothing and subsequent odor as a defense against letting people in. Maybe he was afraid of intimacy and commitment. Maybe I'm projecting all my own stuff onto him, but I highly doubt it.

I'm perfect. I know all of my shadows and I'm completely fixed. I'm never going to feel bad again because I choose not to. And I'm better than everyone else, especially Mr. Thoreau. You can have your Walden, I'm going to buy a Pierre Carden suit. Then I'm going to apply for a civil service job with the IRS and go after tax evaders. Fuck civil disobedience.

I Remember...
The Dead As They Were

All too often we speak well of the dead. We forget their character flaws and nasty idiosyncrasies and glorify them. "Aunt Ruthy was a saint," someone may say at the funeral. They fail to remember the time Saint Ruthy got drunk at Christmas, started an argument with Uncle Frank, set the kitchen on fire and finally drove the '58 Buick through the front window. We forget about incontinence problems, grand jury investigations and having to go into a witness protection program. And going into the witness protection program with someone who is in denial about their incontinence is a very difficult situation; not that I'd know anything about that. I'm merely speculating.

Today I will remember the dead as they were and be thankful I don't have to have to spend anymore time with a mob stoolie who smelled like urine.

I Have Met...
The Second Coming
Of Christ

I was in the mall shopping at a Gap when I bumped into this guy. I say "Excuse me" and he gets in my face with "You meant to do that." I take a look at this guy and he's wearing a robe and has all this long hair. I say "I said excuse me. It was an accident." Then this clown gets all huffy and yells "I'M THE SECOND COMING OF CHRIST!!! I DEMAND AN APOLOGY!" At this point I lose it and say "Fuck you robe boy, now get out of face before I crucify you." The next thing I know I'm on my knees looking at my hand. It's incredibly pained, missing two fingers and this putrid smell is coming from it. "What the hell did you do?" I ask between sobs.

"I've given you leprosy. Now say you're sorry and I may cure you." He says with this smug grin.
"I'm sorry."
"I don't believe you."
"I'm really really sorry I bumped into you."
"Now ask me to cure you"
"Will you please cure me?"
"With sugar on top?"
"Will you please cure me, with sugar on top?"
"Who's your favorite savior?"
"The Buddha."
"What!"
"Just joking, you are."
And then he's gone in a flash of light, my hand is restored and I'm on the floor of a Gap crying. What an asshole.

I Have...
A Sense Of Humor

Since you are reading this page it is obvious you have found offense with one of the vignettes. Personally I am shocked. These writings were written to soothe the soul of everybody on the planet. I have written about the basic human humors that are transcendent of race, religion, political affiliation, gender, sexual orientation and hair color. However, I see I must remind you of the nature of this writing.

IT'S ... A ... JOKE!

As defined by the Random House College Dictionary :

joke n., v., joked, jok.ing –n.
1. a short humorous anecdote with a punch line.

2. anything said or done to provoke laughter or cause amusement.

3. something amusing or ridiculous: I don't see the joke in that.

4. an object of laughter or ridicule, esp. because of being inadequate or sham.

5. a matter not of great seriousness; trifling matter: The loss was no joke.

6. something not presenting an expected challenge; something very easy : The test was a joke.

7. practical joke. –v.i.

8. to speak or act in a playful or merry way.

9. to say something in fun or teasing rather than in earnest: I was only joking. –v.t.

10. to subject to jokes; make fun of; tease.

I Created...
A Vignette

Today I was cruising through the internet when I found a forward to a book about the bars of lower east Manhattan written by Mojo Nixon. Mojo is a funny guy and in the forward he makes the statement, "... he has a better chance of getting head from the Pope before he gets any cash from Mr. No Future." Which I thought was pretty funny.

Well, I thought about this one for a while and began wondering under what circumstances the Pope would give head. Would he wear his big hat? Perhaps the white smoke rising out of the Vatican meant something completely different than what I had been told.

Of course I thought it was fairly funny, if not a bit gross and disrespectful to the Catholic church. Far be it from me to make fun of any organized religion. But I kept going anyway and expanded my thinking to other holy people and saints. I know a few of the gurus out there are charlatans, but there are some who are beyond reproach. Mother Terese popped into my head and I finally had my rhetorical questions.

Under What Circumstances Would Mother Terese

Give The Pope Head? What Would It Look Like?

Personal Note...
I am seriously considering seeking professional help.

I Reduce...
I Reuse...
And I Recycle Humor.

Humor is a finite resource that must be conserved. For far too long we have exploited our humor producing regions. This cannot go on. We must begin today to preserve our humor and the best way is to enjoy old humor.

Steve Martin's Cat Handcuffs is a brilliant piece of comedy that could be enjoyed today instead of shamelessly exploiting the "Redneck" jokes of Jeff Foxworthy. When was the last time you took "The Non–Conformist's Oath?" What about old Bill Cosby routines? His classic album *To My Brother Russel*, Who *I've Slept With* could easily be laughed at to today, sparing us mediocre Jello commercials with the same set of dwarves pretending to be children we've seen for years. How about Andy Griffith's comedy album? Or Bob Newhart's album The Button *Down Bob Newhart* which was the longest album at number one until Michael Jackson's *Thriller* displaced it. Or any of Monty Python's albums, television shows or movies could be humorous today. Hell, some people might even find *Nancy* cartoons funny. Although they're probably too busy listening to Rush Limbaugh to care about comics.

So please, please, please, please, please. Recycle your humor. Please. A punch line is a terrible thing to waste.

I Make Myself...
More Attractive To Women
By Meditating

Man I'm tellin' you, chicks dig guys who meditate. They go for the cool, serene presence a meditative dude brings with him. It's irresistible. Okay, say you're at a bar and want to meet someone. Casually mention Thak Nict Hanh, transcendental meditation, the microcosmic orbit or the Self Realization Fellowship. They come crawling out of the wood work. "Tell me about the higher states of consciousness," they say. "How do you deal with energy blockages in your body," a question most often posed by women who are interested in sharing energy via a mutual microcosmic orbit. I'm tellin' you, meditate and you can't miss.

72

I Use...
Spiritual Pick–Up Lines

Here is a compilation of pick–up line most likely to be used by someone who is "spiritual."

1. I love your energy.
   or
   I love your aura.

2. I know we've only known each other a short time, but I feel like I've known you forever. We must have been lovers in a past life.

3. This one coined by Ram Dass...
   "Would you like to come up and see my altar."

4. I meditate.

5. It must be karma.

   Hope this helps.

I Honor...
Spiritual Commandos

Captain Jensen...This mission is being entrusted to you, the United States' finest spiritual commandos. It is of critical importance that this mission is completed secretly and success-fully. From now on refer to each other only by your code–names. Here is Lieutenant John the Baptist to continue this briefing.

Lieutenant John the Baptist...This grove of trees is our objec-tive. As you can see from the aerial photograph it is an ideal location for this mission. Note the old trees, the pristine river, the grove of samplings and intelligence informs us that there are many rocks, grandmothers and grandfathers as they will be referred to for the rest of the mission, in the area. All the ele-ments are there. Let's check responsibilities. Sergeant Jesus Christ what are your tasks?

Sergeant Jesus Christ...Sir, I am responsible for coordination of the building of the lodge. I and my assistant, Private Mahatma Ghandi, will select the trees for lodge poles. In accor-dance with the protocols we will ask their permission before cutting them down and I have the sage and sanctified ties that will be used to hold the lodge poles together. Also, I have the canvases we will be using to cover the lodge.

Lieutenant John The Baptist...Private Joan of Arc what are your particulars?

Private Joan of Arc…Sir, I am responsible for collecting the fire wood, placing the grandmothers in the fire pit, lighting and tending the fire and carrying the rocks to the lodge during the sweat. I have sharpened my axe and located down wood from the photographs.

Lieutenant John the Baptist…Private, stay out of the fire this time.

Private Joan of Arc…Sir?

Lieutenant John the Baptist…It's a joke. Corporeal Black Elk?

Corporeal Black Elk…Sir, my responsibilities include procuring the water that will be used during the sweat. This includes the pouring water and the drinking water. I have secured a non–metallic ladle and the sacred herbs; sage, sweetgrass, cedar and bear root.

Lieutenant John The Baptist…It's Private Mother Theresa's responsibility to lead the sweat and pour the water. She is currently meditating and seeking guidance from Spirit. She will meet us at the chopper at 0700 hours.

We will depart via helicopter at 0730 and jump into the purification site at 0830. From the moment we hit the ground to the moment we are done with the sweat lodge we will be on Indian time. That means we will be done when we are done. Any questions? Good. Now let's move out and don't forget to check your smudge.

I Beg

Please discover me.

I've been compared to Brad Pitt in looks, a cat in movement and a lunatic in humor. I have an incredible dynamic range, can program a computer, use a can opener, speed break three boards with a punch and write somewhat humorous prose. If all these skills, talents and abilities don't add up to STAR I don't know what does.

I Distinguish...
Between Agape
And Hanging Out

A gape is unconditional love. Some may call it brotherly love. I think of it as wishing well for everyone. It is an ideal state of being I am striving towards. Hanging out is what I do with people who's company I enjoy. I do not wish to hang out with everyone. Nor could I. However, it is an important distinction I needed to learn.

After I first learned about agape, it was a foreign concept until about five years ago, I thought I had to like spending time with everyone. I cannot count the number of times I beat myself up because I wasn't enjoying someone's company. The thought that ran through my head was "I must not love this person unconditionally because I find them annoying, boring and stupid. I'm an awful person." This would lead to the inevitable shame spiral which was finally resolved by being in agape from a distance and hanging out with only people I like.

I Distinguish Between... Oral Sex And Anger Work

A friend is beginning a sexual relationship with his girlfriend. He says they are taking it slow. So far they have talked more than boinked and last night she told him something interesting, "I would really like to give you a blowjob, but I'm afraid my anger issues might come up."

Let me say this, anger work is the last thing I want to have any woman contemplating while per-forming oral sex with me. I'm also a little curious how the two could be confused. In all the anger work I've done, and I have done a lot, there has never been any mouth to genital contact. Okay, there was the one time, but I don't think it's appropriate to write about it here, and besides it was a huge misunderstanding. If for no other reason, I know I can distinguish between oral sex and anger work. I hope you can too.

I Remember...
Losing My Virginity

For some of us losing our virginity is a magical event, a landmark. For some of us it's less than magical. And for some of us it takes far too long to figure how to lose that which we do not want. For good or ill I belong to the latter group, although I didn't actually lose my virginity; I gladly gave it away. And boy was I due. I don't know the precise statistics, but I would say the demographic of twenty–nine year old male virgins is pretty small. I wouldn't be surprised if I was one of less than ten.

"Was" is the operative word. Past tense. History. No longer true. I finally know what sex is like. It is very pleasurable and fun. Especially receiving felatio. Heck, I always thought felatio would be a cool thing and the reality of it was much better than my imagination.

For all those twenty–nine year old male virgins out there, I strongly suggest getting laid and receiving felatio. It really is enjoyable. For the non–twenty–nine year old male virgins reading this, either remember what it was like when you lost your virginity or imagine what it will be like.

I Like ...
"Dr. Bronner's Magic Soap"

Specifically I really like the peppermint soap. Why? Because it makes my scrotum tingle in a very cool way. I highly recommend it.

I Finally Respect...
The Catholic Church

We here at the Catholic church have something important to say. We are wrong. We see now that we cannot speak for Christ and/or God, and honestly we haven't been able to sort out that whole Holy Trinity. Our policies regarding birth control, abortion and real–estate are wrong. We apologize for any inconvenience this may have caused.

Have a nice day,

The Pope

I'm A Little Thin...
On Ideas Today

One Dozen Eggs

Pasta

A loaf of bread

Yogurt

Bananas

Potatoes

Greens

Rice

I'm Going To Kill...
My Roommate

I'm learning to carry a pipe in Lakota tradition. I take the honor and responsibility very seriously. The pipe is a sacred altar. It remembers every prayer ever said into it. Every time it is smoked all the prayers are reissued and carried by the smoke up to Great Spirit. That is why I am going to kill my roommate.

This asshole took my pipe because he broke his water bong and smoked a nickel bag with his friends. My pipe is now ruined. The energy has been completely poisoned and this prayer has probably been entered. "Dude, I am so wasted. You got any salsa to go with these chips?" I don't think Great Spirit wants to hear this every time the pipe is smoked.

Duct Tape Is God

1. God can do anything.

2. Empirically duct tape can do anything.

3. Since two all powerful beings can not exist in this universe at the same time, duct tape must be God.

* The proof of God being duct tape was found by Jim Butler, Doctor of Philosophy.

I Want...
To Pick Your Nose

I am currently studying Rolfing and there is a move where the Rolfer sticks their finger up the sinus passages of the client. It is very interesting to experience this. My Rolfer did it to me once, I actually paid him for this service, and I've done it to myself ... twice.

Now every time I see a person with a scrunched–up, small face I want to stick my finger up their nose. I know it will help them, I just doubt the strangers I see on the street with clogged sinus passages would allow me to. I can't really blame them, but I can have my dreams can't I?

I Believe
"His butt could beat me up!"

How often have you said something like that? If you're like my friend Chris, probably very frequently. Chris made this statement about twelve years ago as we were watching *The Terminator* for the first time with a group of friends. The comment was related to Arnold Schwarzenegger's gluteus maximus, which was quite ripped and huge.

Let's face it. If anybody's butt could beat someone up it would be Arnold's. One quick clench of his cheeks would probably end it for most mortals. I'll bet he could have cracked walnuts in his mighty crack. If for no other reason he deserves the title of best bodybuilder ever.

I Kid You Not

"Hi, you've reached the ecologically sound, harmonically balanced and spiritually centered dwelling of Grazing Tick. I'm either out of the house or out of my body at the moment and can't get to the phone. So please leave a message at the *om*. If you've called for Great Spirit then hang up and listen. Ommmm"

The funny part is that I actually found the entry Great Spirit in the telephone book and called to find out who would answer. Boy was I surprised.

Moving Sucks!

I spent all of today moving and it sucks. Boxing up all my stuff sucked, making sure the room was clean sucked, figuring out what was and wasn't needed sucked and carrying all of my things sucked.

While I'm on a negative note I may as well continue. I hoped to carry a strong and positive tone throughout this year cycle of affirmations, but I've blown it after seven days. So as long as I'm blowing it, I may as well blow it big time.

Life isn't about affirmations for me. I have a hard time taking them seriously, although I do think not beating nuns is a good idea, and there are some things that simply shouldn't be affirmed. Moving is one of these.

Basically I wish I could throw away all of my old things when I decide to live somewhere else and that they'd be magically reproduced at my new dwelling. Alternately I wish I had enough money to pay someone else to move my stuff. That is probably not going to happen in the near future. So here is a guided meditation.

You have decided to move, picture your current abode. Notice all the knick–knacks, clothes, utensils, electronic equipment and the things "you can't live without." They all have to be packed. Now time speeds forward, it is a few days before the big move. There are boxes strewn about the rooms, decisions are waiting for you and the packing is slow. More time passes and less sleep occurs. The day of the move arrives and now picture yourself hauling box after heavy box of stuff. Feel your muscles ache as you lift, push, prod and maneuver your porcelain Elvis collection into your vehicle. Picture yourself making thirty trips in your 1974 VW Beetle. Now picture yourself with all of your crud filled boxes in your new home, all having to be unpacked.

There is no doubt about it, MOVING SUCKS!!!

I Am...
A Talentless Fool

Sometimes the creative juices just don't flow. I haven't had any inspiration for affirmation today so this entry sucks. But that's okay. It's not working perfectly and I know this serves some purpose in my life. I just don't know what.

I Don't Like Call Waiting

I really don't like call waiting. It is an unproven technology with possibly carcinogenic side effects, at least I think so. Well, maybe it doesn't cause cancer, but it sure can cause a lot of stress. What I hate the most is wondering whether the person who is waiting will be there when I click over.

The real question is how long do I press the button for? They say "Just click it," but sometimes when I click it, I click it too fast and I stay on the same line. Usually all I hear is the other receiver being put down, followed by a dial tone. After that it is time to call back the person who was put on call waiting. And usually their phone is busy because they were on call waiting and don't know they've been disconnected. Or, the other extreme, I click it for too long and instead of getting the person on call waiting I get a dial tone.

This call waiting thing is a no win situation. Sure it can allow for two calls to be dealt with at the same time, but it isn't possible to hold two conversations at the same time. So what call waiting really does is put pressure on me to finish one call just so I can click for an inappropriate amount of time and disconnect myself. All in all I think it is a telephone company scheme to make people use their phones more.

My solution was to not have call waiting installed on my telephone. If the call is important, they'll call back. Still, I hate wondering whether I've missed an important call. Damn AT&T.

THIS BOOK WON'T HELP YOU

I Hope Melissa Ethridge... Gets Counseling

There is no doubt about it, Melissa Ethridge is a great singer songwriter. Unfortunately when I listen to her lyrics all I can wonder is is she ever going to have a decent relationship. Along with wondering comes the hope she will get herself into counseling.

"No one loves you like I do."

"But will she die for you like I do?"

It seems like all her songs are about how deeply she is love with somebody and how they treat her like shit. Now I'm not sure, no I'm absolutely sure, I don't want to be involved with anyone who is going to show how much they love me by dying, "Does she die for you like I do?." Perhaps she's one of these people who believes in one of the world's truly evil concepts, soul mates (please add a sarcastic tone). If she is, I suppose I can better understand her lyrics. Whatever the case, I think we all need to help Melissa. Here is a meditation to foster healing in her life.

Find a comfortable position and begin relaxing. Follow each breath inside and with each inhale say to yourself "I am ... relaxed." With each exhale say "I hope Melissa Ethridge gets the counseling she so desperately needs. May she examine her co–dependent tendencies and find a way to love people in a healthy and nurturing fashion while meeting her wants and needs cleanly. By cleaning I mean by asking for what she wants clearly and determining several options for obtaining those

needs." This one may need to be split between several exhales.
Once you feel relaxed begin to imagine Melissa walking into
the counselor's office. See her dealing with her dental floss
issues. See her becoming more and more confident in her relationships. Imagine the lyrics she'll write once she's cured of this
insidious cancer called
co–dependency. For
example "No one sets
boundaries like I do"
or "I can support
you well and in a
healthy manner as
you work through
this wonderful
process called
life."
Why
in no
time
at all
she'll be anoth-
er Amy Grant.
Now there's a well
adjusted female singer
songwriter.

I Question Who 'They' Are

Just who the hell are "they"? You know, they killed JFK, they were responsible for the Persian Gulf War, they put fluoride in the water, they continue the welfare system, and they canceled Star Trek. Bottom line: I want more information.

For once I would like a group of people to claim to be they. I'd even settle for a numerical counting of they. Perhaps there is something like 512 of them. Or is "they" everyone who isn't me or someone I know? That's a staggering thought because there are so many more of them than me, or the occasional us.

I also wonder if there is any way for me to become one of the them. Is there a special they school? They go there and learn how to be one of them. After they're done they conduct surveys, respond to surveys, plot wars with the pentagon, control the liberal and conservative media and hatch fiendish plots. It is staggering how prevalent and invisible they are. It's like I'm trapped in George Orwell's 1984. If anyone knows how to become one of them please let me know.

I Think Sir Isaac Newton...
Was An Asshole

T he world would be a better place if Newton had kept his mouth shut. Just because of an apple falling on his head he invented the field of mathematics known as calculus. If that weren't bad enough he then went on to invent physics because he wanted to explain things. This has given rise to other fields of studies including engineering, computer science and anthropology.

Do we really need to know what pi is to the 100th digit? Is it necessary to understand shear forces in an axle? Does any one really care what Neolithic man looked like? And was it extremely necessary for me to have studied calculus, engineering, device physics and read the Far Side? The answer to all these questions is NO. Except for the Far Side. I suppose anthropology can be forgiven because something funny came out of it. But as to others I lay the blame squarely on Izzy's shoulders.

How much mental anguish has he inflicted on the human race by developing his apple explaining system? It is incalculable. Thousands, no millions, of students throughout the years have labored under his misguided and silly interpretation of the universe. Look at me. I studied a lot of those things and now I'm trying to write an affirmation book. I promise you will not find one derivative, integral or gravitational constant in this writing. Obviously Mr. Newton did not see things very clearly.

I Hate...
Stupid French Clichés

From the nation that gave the world Napoleon, croissants, French bread and a really cool revolution come some of the most moronic clichés. Let's face it, *C'est la Vie* has to be one of the most ridiculous sayings. Such is life. Bullshit.

Maybe in France when someone gets their leg removed in a threshing accident they chuckle amongst themselves and say *"C'est la Vie."* Maybe there that's enough and everyone goes off for a bottle of wine singing cute rounds while the poor amputee bleeds to death. But it doesn't work that way in the good ol' U S of A. We'd say "Holy shit, Vern just got his leg cut off!" And then call 911. Afterwards there'd be no chuckling or singing at the bar where we'd drink beer. Anybody who would say something as stupid as *c'est la vie* would be tossed out the bar on their ass. Obviously that French cliché doesn't work here.

Close your eyes now. With each inhale say "I am relaxed." With every exhale say *"C'est la Vie* is a stupid fucking cliché." Feel the relaxation deepen along with your intolerance for insipid clichés. Picture yourself beating the next person who uses a cliché like "It's raining cats and dogs" with your tire iron; unless it's a nun. When you feel completely relaxed and intolerant return to normal consciousness.

I Believe...
Self-Help Books Are Evil

T here are only a few forms of pure evil on the planet; Michael J. Fox – The Anti–Elvis, any Chicago Bears team that beats the Green Bay Packers and self–help books. I sometimes think self–help books do more harm than good because most use absolutes. Men do this absolutely because of that, where "this" can be anything from premature ejaculation to car maintenance and "that" ranges from unresolved childhood sexual incidences involving an iguana to the oil needs changing. Or, women without question do such–and–such because of this–and–that. "Such–and–such" might be wear make–up and "this–and–that" varies from wanting to look good so they feel an intense insecurity caused by the male dominated hegemony which forces them to be slaves to their bodies and looks; depending on how angry the author is. The point is, nobody can know absolutely how or why everyone will react in a given situation. Ultimately I believe self–help books cause more problems than they solve.

I believe most of these authors, while well intentioned, are unwilling to claim their ideas. So here is a suggestion. Go through every self–help book you can find and look for the words that identify large segments of the population, i.e. men, women, us, we, they, them. When you encounter one of these vast generalizations change it to I and see what insights you get on the authors. With this simple technique I have been able to more clearly see that self–help gurus are simply stating their opinions, not universal truth.

Man, I Don't...
Understand Feminists

Like you know, I was hangin' out on the co'ner wit' Joey and Eddy and Franky. And we was discussin' Dostoevsky's The Brother's Karamotzov. Now you know, it is a fine work of literature. But, the beginning can be rather long and tedious. So we was talkin' about dat.

So you know like Joey thought the beginning really detracted from the overall psychological impact of the story. He just couldn't, I don't don't know, really keep his attention on the action after being inundated with all this genealogy. And I agreed, it is difficult to keep one's attention on the story after such boring beginnings. But, I found the plot line later to very engaging. And Franky started talkin' about how the translation from Russian to English has to have the idiosyncrasies of the time period explained because, you know, those are very important for people who have not studied Russian history. While as he was arguing about the poor historical content of the translation we read when this beautiful woman walked by.

I could not help myself and so I says to her I says "Excuse me. But you is one beautiful chyck."

Oh and she all upset and says "You pig. How can you call me chick? I am a woman, not an object or a small bird."

And I says "No, you do not understand. I said chyck with a y. That means I know you are a beautiful, sensitive woman who has an emotional side and spiritual beauty. It is a term of honoring. You see, your physical beautiful is but the merest reflection of your soul. I know you are creature of the universe; divine and immortal. And you also got a great raq."

She listened to my explanation, but when I told her she had a great raq she turned walked away without sayin' a word. She didn't even give the chance to explain the biblical significance of the term.

So you see, I just don't understand feminists.

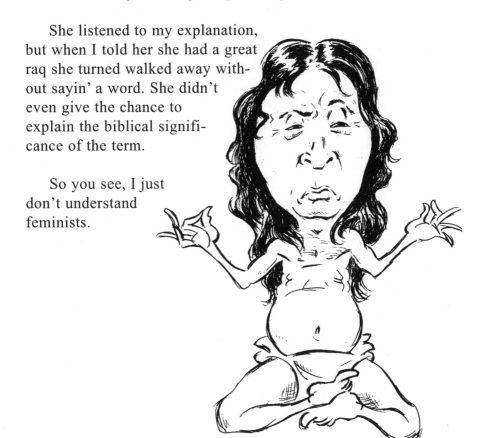

THIS BOOK WON'T HELP YOU

I Am Grounded, Centered And Still Confused

I have been chakraed, Peaceful Warriored, shamaned, meditated, Tai Chied, therapied (regular, transcendental and extra–crispy), sensory deprivated, New Warriored, Shadow Worked, Miracle of Loved and I still don't know what I'm going to do with my life. Despite being centered and grounded I'm still working as a courier, don't have an intimate relationship and haven't been able to find a decent eight track tape player in years.

Sure, I can still find a few broken ones and fix them. It's just that the reproduction quality isn't good. All my favorite songs are distorted and I hate to hear my Saturday Night Fever soundtrack in poor fidelity. And all the groundedness and centeredness won't change that. So what good is this New Age crap?

I bought into the myth. Look at personal issues, discharge them in a safe place and use the new emotional technologies to transform my life. Well it ain't working. People still think I'm strange, my family has disowned me and I can't even explain some of the New Age things I've done, let alone been transformed. It's all a money scam, I say. The weirder the shit they want you to do the more they charge. Well I've had enough. From now on the only thing I want to hear from a so–called guru is "I've got a new eight track tape player for you."

I Am Cautious...
Of People
With Flaky New Age Names

A lot of good has come from the New Age. Yoga, meditation, emotional processing technologies, the rethinking of parenting, and incense are just some of the marvels I can tout. Unfortunately an incredibly stupid and flaky trend also found birth there. Names.

One of my tenets of life is to stay away from people with flaky names. Without a doubt the weirder the name, the weirder the person. I once met a woman named Translucent Whisper who convinced me to take malted milk enimas, that sucked. Nova Rising wanted to have a three hour chanting session before fixing his flat tire. He interpreted the flat as a sign from God that he was acting from ego instead of his heart. I took it as a sign he should buy new tires, they were all bald. And finally there was Grazing Tick.

I met Grazing Tick at a men's retreat weekend. He was way into Native American Indian spiritual practices and had received his name in a vision after fasting for four days on a mountain. Well the first thing I said after being introduced to him was "You better stay away from my dog." Then I pulled out my lighter to see if he'd retreat from the heat of the flame. Nearly got into a fight over that one. Flaky New Age people, especially one's with weird names, rarely have a sense of humor.

I Will Pay My Bills

I'm in big trouble. I let a credit card slip for too long and now a collection agency is after me. I think they mean business.

Alexander The Great Collection Agency
"We treat dead beats like the Gordium Knot"

Dear Sir,

Recently we have received a request from "Fred's Bank Credit Card" to attempt collection of your delinquent account, numbered 15. It appears you haven't made a payment on the outstanding debt of $5,439.52 in the past six months.

We will, of course, start garnishing your wages. In the event you do not have a job we have already located your apartment and will be stealing anything we deem valuable. If these two methods fail to balance your account we will be forced to resort to murder.

This may seem rather cruel, and I assure you it is simply a long standing company policy, but your memory will live on as a constant reminder to those people who do not properly manage their money. We currently have three choices of death available. The first is a Colombian Necktie. The second method of death is an execution style bullet to the base of the neck. The third method, and the most popular, is to be drawn and quartered. Regardless of the method you choose, your head will be erected on a spike outside our office buildings where birds will feast on it for two to three weeks.

Thank you in advance for your cooperation. Have a nice day.

Sincerely,

Jacob Smiley, Collection Director

I Use...
My Blinkers!

O kay all you people who have blue hair, or smoke a pipe and drive or wear a baseball hat, especially backwards, and have a bumper sticker like Coed Naked Bullfighting: Getting gored was never so much fun, or anyone in the Chicago area here's today's affirmation. *Use your fucking blinkers. It's easy.* Pull the little lever on the left side of the steering column down when you want to turn left and push it up when you want to turn right.

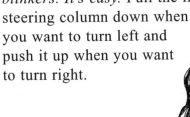

I Immortalize...
My Neighbor With Poetry

The Hyena Laughs

She's actually my next door neighbor

But sometimes I hate her

Late at night her voice crashes through my door like a bullet

Whaa ha ha ha ha ha

piercing shrill loud nasty evil bad voice

The worst part is

it's as fake as plastic fruit

Forced constricted and loathsome

Ooh I could never live with this woman

I'd have to cut out her larynx

It would be self defense

I Am Wary Of Fanatics

Some fanatics are easy to spot. They call themselves republicans, democrats, Born Again Christians, the NRA or Packer Fans; to name a few. However, there are other types of fanatics which are more subtle but no less deadly. I have a few tips to help you spot them.

First there is the Panacea Attitude. "If everybody would do what I/we do the world would be fixed." This one is nasty. If every person would learn how to chop wood, carry water and do Zen meditation then nuclear waste would go away. Right. It would be nice if that were the case, but I doubt it.

Second, there is the "I was garbage before I started doing this and now I've been fixed" myth. This is a big one. Talk to anyone who has been part of a twelve step process. Talk about non–acceptance of life events. They may not remember much of their co–dependent/dysfunctionally related coping mechanistic time, but that doesn't negate its importance. Who can say which step while walking a mile is the most valuable?

Third is the attitude, especially if you leave, that "You can't live without us." This smacks of cult think to me and I base this one on actually being involved briefly with an organization that was later identified as a cult. They were fucking weird and whenever I hear anything with the implication "You can't live without us" I know they are fanatics.

So why is fanaticism something to be wary of? It all boils down to a basic non–exploration of life, stagnation. If a group or person purports to have all the answers to life, why look elsewhere, why explore; in fact why even live at all? In my humble opinion the only panacea for life is life.

I Understand...
Fanatical Quotes

I just saw this one and had to point it out as a fanatical quote. "Just write. Say yes, stay alive, be awake. Just write. Just write. Just write." This is from Natalie Goldberg's *Writing Down the Bones*. Much of her writing drones on about keeping the hand moving, don't think, just write fast, don't worry about what you write. Well as far as I'm concerned she's a writing/Buddhist fanatic. If I read another quote from Katagiri Roshi, a Zen master – big hairy deal (perhaps he's a big, hairy Zen master), translated into writing wisdom I'm going to mindfully shred the book into tiny pieces.

Back to the quote above. The implication seems to be that whoever you are the only way to say yes, the only way to stay alive, the only way to be awake is to write. What horseshit.

Take this to heart. If the only time I am alive is when I'm writing then the only time I'm alive is when I'm alone, sitting at a word processor hoping the trash I produce will mean something to someone else. That's a small, miserable world to be alive in. Natalie, I'll be alive all the time if you don't mind. Of course, being Jewish, you might.

I Offend...
Everybody

I've offended everybody. I've offended democrats, republicans, feminists, fanatics, Elvis fans, Michael J. Fox, Michael J. Fox fans, Jesus, Buddha, Natalie Goldberg, collection agents who don't kill their debtors, people who don't use their blinkers, Jews, Christians, Hindus and God. I know I have. Oh everybody please forgive me, I didn't mean to. It was all an accident. The devil made me do it. I was so victimized by my parents that I had to act out, it's their fault. Society oppressed me so much that I finally lashed out at those institutions I deemed responsible. Please, it'll never happen again.

I Hate Pennies

And I don't mean Penny Marshall. I mean that insignificant form of currency. Maybe in old Ben Franklin's day a penny saved was a penny earned, but in these times a penny saved is pocket trash. Who cares about pennies? I can't think of a single thing I can buy with a penny. Even penny candy costs at least three cents. It is all a government conspiracy to weight us down with useless baggage. Fuck pennies.

Of course, I mean that in a figurative sense. It would be damn difficult to have a satisfying sexual experience with a penny, Lord knows I've tried, you need at least a fifty cent piece.

I Protect...
My Ass From The Sun

I sunburned my ass. It's a painful thing to experience and admit. I'll let you guess how I pulled this off and recommend you don't do it yourself.

Oh God, what will people think about my lack of tan lines and the redness where redness has no place being? Right now I'm feeling a lot of shame and have devised a new mantra to help me learn from this issue.

I will not sunburn my ass.

I will not sunburn my ass.

I will not sunburn my ass.
(Repeat as often as necessary)

I Find...
Ducks Clumsy

Today while walking to the gym I noticed a duck flying. It looked like he was going to crash into one of the two houses across the street and as he disappeared I expected to hear a thud and then a muffled quack as the creature hit the ground. It didn't happen and when I got in front of the houses there he was, standing on the roof like a proud sentry. I tried to see the majesty in the pose and failed miserably.

Let's face it, ducks are the brunt of a lot of jokes for a very good reason. They deserve it. The only place a duck looks graceful and at peace is on the water. But walking on land or flying they look like they're doing it for the first time. Have you ever seen a duck land on water? It's like they're guessing at the whole procedure. "Okay, wings out. Yeah, that's good. Ah ah ah ah, feet down, I remember. Where's that damn manual? Angle of descent looks good. Hey! What's that stuff? It's moving. Water, right. All right. All right. All right. I'm ready. LAND!" Then there's a big splash of water as the creature drags to a halt. They always looked surprised that they're still alive. And frankly, so am I.

I Want...
A New Form Of
Representation

Who invented majority rule? Some majority from a long time ago. Why are we still following an outmoded form of government? Why can't we experiment with new forms of government? How about pizza delivery people rule? Or people who have given fruit cakes as Christmas gifts rule, one fruit cake one vote? Or those whose last name has the third letter of "q" are judges? Any woman who can do a hand stand push–up is a Senator. Why are we so stuck on a representative government?

Eight of Steve's Ten Tips... For A Happy Life

1. Always live East of where you work.

2. Never go out with a girl
who has more problems than you do.

3. No woman is ugly with your dick in her mouth.

4. Never defend Europe when playing Risk.

5. Never commit to a ground war in Asia

6. If you meet a girl at a bar and everything
is going too well, she probably likes your friend.

7. Never play pool against a man named Minnesota or
Louisiana or any other geographical location
for a first name.

8. Never bowl against a man who brings his own ball.

Note...Steve is a dear friend of mine. And even though our life philosophies seem to deal with different scopes, I believe his views have validity. Especially # 3.

I Reduce...
My Use Of Profanity

I've been looking over my writing and have noticed a distressing profanity trend. I've been using such evil language as fuck, breast, damn, Sunny Delight and asshole. Sometimes in reference to people and/or holy men. It is stopping here.

From now on all language will be of a clean nature. Fuck will be replaced with gosh darn it, breast with bodacious ta–ta, Sunny Delight with orange shit and damn with shucky darn. However, in the spirit of accurately representing my writing, I will keep the language, no matter how vile and offensive, of the earlier vignettes in tact. I apologize once again for my deplorable use of language and hope you forgive me. If not then you can just fuck right off. Ooops, sorry.

I Look Like...
A Geek When I Workout

Not that I don't look like a geek most of the time anyway. However, when I workout it is especially apparent. Bad pants, ugly shirt, beat up shoes and, worst of all, white tube socks. I'm simply a fashion disaster waiting to happen. I should just wear a pocket protector in the gym and give up trying to look cool.

I Understand...
Introductory
Reincarnation Theory

. . . .
. . . .
 . . . .
. . . .
. . . .
. . . .
. . . .
. . . .
. . . .
. . . .
 .. ^ You are here . . .
. . . .
. . . .
. . . .
. . . .
. . . .
. . . .
. . . .
. . . .
. . . .

Note...each '.' represents a lifetime.

I Am Going To Die

And so are you. Have a nice day.

I Am Learning...
To Date

Perhaps this is misrepresenting my situation. Let's say going on a date for me is like climbing Mount Everest. Now if I can't climb Mount Everest because I can't find it on a map then that's about where I am with dating. I just don't get it.

I have dated in the past. I have actually met women, asked them out and they said yes. One thing led to another and suddenly we were dating. However, I've taken time off from dating, my social circles have grown smaller and it seems like the rules have changed.

First rule. It is illegal to make eye contact with a man you don't know. There are just these little eye flickers followed by the demure "I'm busted" look. Without eye contact it is next to impossible to begin any type of a conversation. They simply go scampering away ashamed that they were noticed noticing.

Second rule. In the event of making eye contact and learning the name of someone new you must ignore them completely later. So far I haven't learned if this one is based on shyness or a passive aggressive leave me alone. All I can say is it's a pisser to actually make the effort to say hello and then be completely ignored later. You know the type of ignoring where you know they know you're there and they ignore you just the same.

I'm not sure what to do. I think I'll keep trying different maps, perhaps a globe. Mount Everest is out there somewhere.

I Am...
Rhythmically Impaired

Every Friday I have a piano lesson. Every Friday my piano teacher Angie conducts a clinic for the rhythmically impaired. My disability with rhythm is most apparent when I try to split a beat into four parts. She first tried the word watermelon, but I didn't get it had four syllables until I got home. We now use "1–e–and–a–2–e–and–a ..." for my rhythmic base. Because I have two degrees in Electrical Engineering I can handle the counting. The real problems begin when clapping is added.

"Clap with the notes," says Angie for the umpteenth time. Like it's that easy. She must think I'm some sort of a rhythmic genius. "Every once in a while I find someone who has bad rhythm [like you] and have to fix them." Angie's statement brings up a lot of questions for me.

Why didn't I have rhythmic lessons earlier on in life? Is it possible for a twenty–nine year old white male to find rhythm, let alone split it into four parts and clap appropriately? Can I sue anyone for my educational deficiencies? Is it the fault of my middle school band director for not allowing me to play the saxophone? Had he let me switch I'm sure I'd have stuck with the band and learned rhythm when I was much younger.

Regardless of class action law suits, I'm devoted to learning the piano, rhythm and all. Someday it's my hope to put it all together. Clapping, counting and, finally, playing with perfect rhythm. I'm just worried about splitting the beat into eight parts. Perhaps hexamethylenetetramine will serve.

I Love...
My Spell Checker

A ny program that can look at the word wisemen and give as an alternative "WI semen" (Wisconsin semen) is okay in my book.

I Pity...
The East
And West Coast Snobs

I'm tired of these East and West coast snobs overlooking, belittling and not knowing where the Midwest is. Honestly, I once had a woman from New York ask "What state is Wisconsin in?" I told her "Wisconsin is a state. It's the land mass north of Chicago." I think the root of her ignorance was Population Envy.

She, like most people who live on the coasts, was envious of the middle states because we have so much room. They envy how low our population density is and make fun of our life style to mask their desire to live in the land of Cheeseheads, Fibs, and cow tipping. To help people with Population Envy I have created a meditation.

Close your eyes and breath deep. With each inhale say "I am relaxed." With each exhale say "I am in the midwest." Let the spaciousness of the middle states penetrate your soul. Hear the cows. See the farmers. Notice the absence of crime, pollution and cultural events. Return to normal consciousness when you've had your fill of clean air, low crime and space.

I Honor...
The Real Twelve Days
Of Christmas

On the twelfth day of Christmas the holidays gave to me:

Twelve nervous breakdowns

Eleven fruit cakes

Ten maxed out credit cards

Nine gifts to wrap

Eight screaming kids

Seven knick knacks

Six Christmas specials

Five fish ties

Four dozen cookies

Three pairs of socks

Two candy bars

And a Christmas tree to decorate

I Honor...
My Friend Gordy

My friend Gordy once had a very very profound insight which I carry with me to this day He realized that whenever an ambulance sped past him with the siren blaring someone was having a worse day than him.

I Understand...
The Dating "Queue"

I'm getting clarity on this dating thing. Not much success, except for getting laid...once. However, we really didn't date that much before or after having sex. It's a long story. Suffice it to say the encounter wasn't, at least I think it wasn't, a "normal" type of occurrence. Enough about my pathetic sex life.

The dating "queue" is a pattern I'm beginning to see. I believe whenever someone is dating they create a queue of potential dates against the possibility of the current relationship vaporizing. My observation with women is that there are three types of queues men can apply for. The first, and largest, is the I–Wouldn't–Spend–Time–With–You–If–You–Were–The–Last–Man–On–Earth queue. The second is the Possible–Date queue. And the final queue is the Pro–Bono–Therapist queue. This is the worst queue for a man to be in.

Signs that you may be in the third queue are...

1. Listening sympathetically to her problems ... for hours.

2. Watching her go through shitty relationship after shitty relationship.

3. The phrase "I'd love to date a guy just like you" quickly followed by

4. The sure sign you are her therapist "but not you. Let's just be friends." If you have experienced any of these signs you may be a Pro–Bono–Therapist. You will only have a shot at a romantic relationship after the first two queues are empty. It is a vast wasteland and I know because I have lived there for years. Get out while you still can.

I Know...
Where To Find Dates

Cruise the male prisons visitor areas. No, it's not what you think. The chicks flock there. Just sit in the waiting room and talk to the women as they come to visit. You can use this sure–fire line, "My friend's in for drunk driving. What's your man in for?" You know, just go with the flow and bingo, you got a coffee date. Hey, it's gotta be better than the bars and personals.

I Am Amazed At The Limits Of Human Stupidity

Sometimes I just don't know. Here's the picture. I'm on my bike pedaling in a bike lane. This in and of itself is not stupid. The fact that I am doing this when the temperature is −30° Fahrenheight with the wind chill makes this maneuver suspect at best. But the two, idiots is the only word that fits, idiots I saw were off the scale.

The first guy was wearing a jean jacket. Wearing a jean jacket in this kind of weather to keep warm is like using mosquito netting to stop a Terminator. He had on no gloves. He had on no hat. I could only laugh and ask "Why?" as I biked past this Wisconsin yeti.

The second guy was round. Portly. Picture the Stay Puff Marshmelow Man crossed with the Michellen Man. He was bopping over the frozen tundra without a hat or gloves. He was wearing a leather jacket ... which was three–quarters unzipped. A red sweater showed and all I could think was this guy had a nuclear reactor for a power supply. Anything else would have frozen solid.

Sometimes I just don't know about the residents of Wisconsin. Not to slam them, they are wonderful, friendly people, but they just don't respect the elements. It's not uncommon for Packer fans to go shirtless at the last home game of the season. Nevermind the wind–chill, frostbite and possible amputations possible because of this behavior. One clown of this ilk, on a dare, wore shorts throughout the winter. He froze his ass off for four months. And for what? Probably a case of Point beer.

The limits of human stupidity continue to amaze me.

Cynicisms

(This Affirmation unintentionally left blank.)

Woolite Cold Water Wash

*ph balanced to clean and protect without
shrinking, stretching or fading.*

Trust Woolite to safely and effectively clean the washable
clothes you care about – blouses, lingerie, activewear,
pantyhose, sweaters, baby clothes and more! Great for
washables of silk cotton, wool, cashmere, polyester, acrylic,
nylon, rayon and other synthetics.

MACHINE WASHING...
Gentle or delicate cycle recommended. Select the cold water
setting, add 1/4 cup Woolite – that's half as much as ordinary
detergents – and then add garments. Contains 16 machine washes.

HAND WASHING...
Fill cap to line and pour into sink. Then add cool or cold water.
(Use more for larger sinks, less for smaller sinks.) Soak garments for 3 minutes. Gently squeeze suds through. Rinse thor-
oughly in cool or cold water. Roll in towel to remove excess
water. Do not wring or twist. Dry flat, away from sun and heat.
Contains up to 80 hand washes.

I Think...
You're All Scum

I've thought about my last affirmation and decided I don't care. You're all scum. Go fuck yourselves. If you're not willing to accept me and my humor then just go the fuck away. I don't need this shit in my life. If I want to compare Parmahansa Yoganonda and John Lovitz then I will. If I think fanatics are dangerous then I'll say that. If you don't like it, put my book down. Use your own discretion. Don't just mindlessly read my writing and get upset by it; put it away, shred it up, burn it. Do whatever you want with it, just don't lay this "You've offended me" garbage on me. Deal

I Improve...
Shakespeare

Shakespeare had all this talent and he wasted it on plays and sonnets. Not that his stuff isn't good, it can be entertaining sometimes, but it is missing something. And that something is sex.

Sure there always seems to be a cross–dresser running around in a play, but never a direct reference sex, orgasms or genitalia. Simple rewriting would have improved Shakespeare incredibly, as you can see below.

Hark. What sound through yonder window floats?
Is it the coming of the dawn, or Juliet coming?

Romeo...
A lay by any other name would still leave a wet spot.

With just a little revision of context Lady MacBeth's line, "Out damn Spot", would be perfect.

Shakespeare once said, "The play is the thing with which I'll catch the conscience of the King." He would have done better to catch the King's libido.

I Am Inspired To Work Less

You moron! Why the hell are you so busy? Can't you see it's killing you. All the stress, all the pressure, all the tension. And for what? A raise? A house? A car? Keeping your kids fed? You're a fool. Look at yourself. You're a neurotic mess, always looking over your shoulder for the next big deal or co–worker who's going to stab you in the back. It's not that tough to be peaceful. Take a vacation. Write meditations. Reduce your responsibilities. Listen to Abba albums. There's a whole world of relaxation possibilities. Use them.

I Appreciate This Special
Message From My Family

What?
Can't you read their minds?

I Integrate...
The Four Habits
Of Colossally Useless People

1. Procrastination.

2. Renewing fear of success and failure.

3. Total and complete lack of personal responsibility.

4. Collect Elvis statuettes.

Editor's Note...
A book is forthcoming. It will detail
how to acquire and hone these habits.

I No Longer Make Sexual References

The hallmark of low–brow humor is referring to sex. I'm better than that and I will no longer stoop to such depths. No longer will you have to endure such sexually explicit phrases as penis, vagina, breasts and groceries. There will be no further reference to male masturbation hidden in the euphemisms whacking the worm, lubricating the pole, squeezing the Charmin or carrying groceries. Furthermore I promise to refrain from any illusion to female masturbation such as riding the electric pogo stick, embracing a cucumber, good vibrations or getting a shopping cart. In the future I will simply look to the comic genius contained in Bazooka Joe Bubble Gum and Nancy cartoons for inspiration.

I Wish...
I Were Black

Every summer it's the same. Burn, peel, burn, peel, burn, burn, burn, burn, peel and then tan. If I'm lucky. And these men and women of color simply have it. I wish I was black. I could walk around with dark and beautiful skin instead of looking like some shriveled, white maggot eight months out of the year. It's not fair. My skin color should have no bearing on how well I tan. I'm being oppressed by my genes. Oppressed. I'm going to sue my parents for giving me horrible chromosomes, it's their fault I am at risk of skin cancer. Of course, if I were black I'd have to worry about sickle cell anemia. Can nothing be simple?

THIS BOOK WON'T HELP YOU

I Listen...
To The Arch–Angel
Tremendoolengsplat

I, the great Tremendoolengsplat, am speaking today through the conscious channeling of Translucent Whisper. This woman, who through her diligent pursuit of higher vibrational consciousness and enemas, has become a willing transmitter of my Universal Wisdom. All pay homage to the humble Translucent Whisper. Oh yes, she also informs me the homage that would be most appreciated is cash. Please mail it to Translucent Whisper. She's late with her rent.

I have made my presence known because there is a wonderful event on the horizon, the opening of the Cosmic Sluice Gate. When this happens, in the very near future give or take a decade, the consciousness of the entire planet will be raised to such a point that God's Angelic Host, led by me, will become visible. I have come to prepare you for the awakening. This awakening will be particularly difficult for the unconscious unknowing who do not follow my teachings. They will hear angels are coming and think that beautiful creatures will be visible. Nothing could be farther from the truth.

For all of human history we have deliberately lied to humanity. We are ugly. Hideously ugly. And we lied to you because you would not have trusted us if you knew we make the Elephant Man look like Tom Cruise. Actually, the Elephant Man was part of the Angelic Host incarnated on earth to help awaken innate abilities in all humans. But did he get a chance? No! You humans couldn't look past his unusual looks and branded him an outcast. He could have been a great leader. But what did you do? You threw him out of society, kept his bones and eventually sold them to Michael Jackson. For that alone God was pretty pissed. Things have cooled since then and now the time has arrived, possibly, for you to see the nature of the Universe, and it isn't as pretty as you think.

The Great Tremendoolengsplat has spoken; and don't forget to send money to Translucent Whisper.

I Want People Who Make Incorrect Prophesies Punished

I am tired of these twinkies who profess to see the future and make predictions that are wrong. It isn't that the predictions are bad in and of themselves, it is just that the track record of most of these idiots is awful and yet they get away with delivering wrong messages year after year. What I propose is that the business of prophesy be regulated like the Yakuza.

Whenever one of these twinkasourases makes a wrong prediction two "Dutch Cousins" show up and cut off a finger at the knuckle. The way I see it a prophet gets twenty–eight strikes. It seems fair, and let me explain why.

There is a dweeb, in my humble opinion, who has been prophesying that a major calamity will hit the world for nearly eight years. This guy has even drawn maps of what the world will look like afterwards and for some reason I keep thinking about this. And let me tell you, I prophesize that this guy is going to have a broken nose if California isn't a series of islands by the end of this year. Bottom line, I'm sick of worrying about this thing and if he's wrong he's got a lot to answer for. At least three knuckles worth!

I Understand...
The History Of Rugby

A fierce competition where unpadded people hurl them-selves at top speed into other unpadded people for the sake of a ball. It is the predecessor of war. Here, for the first time, is an accounting of the first armed attack.

"Hey Nigel."

"What d' ya want, Ian?"

"I was just thinking. There's a scrum going on and I'd really like to get the ball, but I don't think I'll get anywhere near it. What if I took this here sharp piece of metal and stabbed all the opposing players."

"Say ... that is an idea. And I could take this piece of wood, chain and metal ball with spikes and fashion some sort of a ... I don't know ... ball and chain and join you."

"That's the idea. And when we're done we can rape the cheer-leaders."

After this game three teams formed called England, Scotland and Ireland, elected captains and co–captains called kings and nobles, and decided to see who would be the last team standing. It was so much fun that warfare was exported to the entire world and soon rugby followed, but it wasn't as popular.

I Am Pro–Choice...
And I Eat Small Children

I am a wicked witch and I eat naughty small children. I live deep in the old forest in my house made of ginger bread. When naughty, wicked small children get lost in the woods they find my house and are always lured by the sweet, tasty gingerbread. Once they have eaten their fill and can't move I capture them, fatten them and eat them. And I am Pro–Choice.

Even though I derive sustenance and great pleasure from small children I believe it is a woman's right to choose whether she wants to bear a fetus to term. Part of this belief comes from being a woman, although I'd never had a child because I know I'd sauté it in butter, and part of it is self–preservation. With so many children running around because of lack of abortion I believe a lot of people would start eating children and it would become difficult for me to keep my larder filled.

Keep abortion safe and legal. It will keep me from starving.

I Support...
Stephen King Changing
His Writing Premises

Dear Stevey,

I have been reading your books for years and derived many hours of pleasure from them. But, it is time for you to move on. If I read another flyer claiming that the next Stephen King book is the most terrifying one ever I'm going to puke. Let's face it, you have stalked, cornered and beaten into a bloody mess the horror genre.

I'd like to see you write a romance novel or perhaps a comedy. A light hearted buddy picture about two divorced men who have to move in together. And here is the kicker, they're complete opposites. One is incredibly clean and the other is a slob. They'd make a real odd couple. Or maybe a movie about a woman who gets married, has a couple kids, her husband cheats on her and then she dies of cancer. I bet it'd make a great movie and be a real tear jerker.

Those are just a few suggestions. I'm sure given your creativity your can find lots of other topics to write about other than vampires, evil sewer clowns, haunted mansions in Colorado, possessed dry cleaning equipment, kids finding dead bodies and plagues.

Sincerely,

Edgar Allen Poe

I Am Testing
The Emergency Affirmation
System

This is a test of the Emergency Affirmation System. This is only a test.

You're late for work. The kids have the flu. You're just not good enough. You feel like you need to eat a whole quart of Hagen Daaz ice cream. You don't want to go to the gym. You feel like you have no purpose in life. Your Higher Power has abandoned you. Your car won't start. You have a flat. Your favorite television program was canceled and replaced with Laroquette.

If this had been an actual emergency you would have been informed of which affirmation to use, who to hire as a therapist and where the closest grocery store that carries Hagen Daaz is located.

This concludes this test of the Emergency Affirmation System.

140

I Review Species

(Ghandi versus Predator)

A brilliant cinematic masterpiece. Ben Kingsley recreates his role as Ghandi, the spiritual leader of India who leads India to freedom from the British, in a surprising science fiction sequel. In Species Ghandi teams up with four other people to rid Los Angeles of a horny alien that kills a lot of people. The climax of the movie is when Ghandi finally corners the alien.

Ghandi...
I will not harm you. My way is the way of passive resistance. So leave this planet, there is no room for you here. I will sit here and spin cloth until you leave.

Alien...
Growls inarticulately and kills Ghandi.

What a movie. What acting. What a piece of shit.

I Appreciate...

I'll Have A Big Mac,

Large Fries And,

Yes, A Diet Coke.

No, I Do Not Want Cookies

This affirmation is best done in a very "powerful" tone of voice

I Know...
The Real Wedding Vows

Do you take this man to be your lawfully wedded husband?

Do you promise to only ask him a maximum of ten times if you look good before going out?

Do you promise to share your meals at restaurants?

Do you promise to use the phrase "If you really loved me you'd <fill in the blank>" a maximum of three times during any argument? Do you promise to find tasteful knick–knacks for your dwelling?'

Do you take this woman to be your lawfully wedded wife?

Do you promise to reassure her of her looks before going out?

Do you promise to finish her meals at restaurants?

Do you promise to use the phrase 'Of course I love you. I work to buy you <fill in the blank>' a maximum of three times during an argument?

Do you promise to do the heavy manual labor required in your dwelling?'

I Like...
FOX Programming

Rhinelander 54426...

In tonight's premiere episode the Trevish family moves from a wealthy suburb of Boston to their new home in Rhinelander, Wisconsin to begin pig farming. The children begin school and soon find themselves in the middle of controversy. Malcom is ostracized by the middle school boys for not "Backing The Pack" and his inability to say 'Hey Der' properly. Debra doesn't know what a Hodag is and is laughed at by all the girls. But, the trouble really begins when the family asks where the synagogue is. Can these Eastern snobs adjust to the subtle nuances of the midwest, plaid and the odor of pig dung? Tune in tonight at 8:00 PM on Fox to find out.

What Have I Become?

Oh Christ, this affirmation thing has gone way too far. The genesis for the last piece of work was the death of a friend's mother. I didn't even know this woman and when he started telling me about her demise the only thing I could think of was getting him a sympathy card. Then I realized there are no sympathy cards for truly nasty people, not that his mother was nasty in any way shape or form. I mean have you ever seen a card that started with 'I know it's sad, but he really was a smelly incontinent old man.' I'm sure there's a market for this stuff, but why did I have to think this up while my friend was talking? It was all I could do not to burst out laughing. I haven't been the same since I stopped drinking my urine.

I Honor The NOW Woman Of The Year

In a bold and daring move the National Organization of Women has elected the prune to be its woman of the year. When asked why, Ms. Joanne Kickhimintheballs said "What better symbol for modern feminism than the prune? It is one of the few fruits that can be dried without spoiling, is full of vitamins and, to date, has never been used as a tool in a sexual assault. Let's face it, the prune simply screams feminism." While few can argue with the logic, questions were raised as to why other, more human, applicants weren't chosen.

"NOW has a long history of choosing the most crusty, viscous and atheistic feminist as our Woman Of The Year. In looking at the candidates we couldn't find one with sufficiently deep furrows in the face or a level of acidity worthy of the title. Although, Melinda Tortureallthemenjustbecause–daughter came close for her breathtaking feminist historical paper 'Kill All The Men.' Unfortunately her face was too smooth and she actually believes in a higher power.

"Then, our application committee found a ten year old prune sitting in the back of a fruit bin. It was hard as a rock, crusty and when we threw it at a two year old boy it left a deep bruise. We knew we had our Woman Of The Year."

Now that NOW has opened the competition to inanimate crusty objects next year's competition is sure to be intense. Already the stale bread, cow chip and the bubble–gum under the desk lobbies are beginning their campaigns. Until next year's winner is announced, however, the prune will reign as a majestic and craggy representative of the power of feminism.

I Offend Pro-Lifers...
and I Have a Sniper Rifle

We who hold life dear were disgusted to find Mr. Craig Rypstat joking about eating small children. There is nothing funny whatsoever about eating small children, that would be like finding a cream pie tossed in the face funny or the movie Catch–22 entertaining. Nothing could be further from the truth.

How many people have you incited to eat their small children? You underestimate the power of your words. Merely suggesting the consumption of children will cause people to start eating them, just like merely mentioning s–e–x can cause p–r–e–g–n–a–n–c–y.

You will burn in the deepest parts of hell. And if that isn't bad enough we're going to picket your house, take your picture and yell nasty epitaphs at you. And another thing, we'll carry signs showing small children prepared in various ways; i.e. stewed, fricasseed, in a casserole and as soup. So you have been warned. Stop this promotion of eating children or you may find our justice dispensed in the form of a sniper's bullet.

Yours in God's Love,

Those who believe in killing people who joke about killing children

I Believe...
Sunny Delight Sucks

I have tasted Sunny Delight and, in my opinion, I'd rather drink my own urine. This vile, slightly orange tasting, fizzy pseudo liquid will never sell well, regardless of the marketing scheme.

Usually it's cool looking kids (black, white or both) looking into a refrigerator filled with drinks. Suddenly one of them sees Sunny Delight and instead of saying "Look there's Sunny Delight. I'd rather vivisect myself with spoon than drink that swill" they say something stupid like "Hey there's a Sunny, we're set." I'm sure it's meant to sound cool, but it never works. And someone seems to think changing the nickname from Sunny D to plain Sunny will make the product taste better. Here's a hint, It Doesn't. The reason your product sucks is because your product sucks. Why don't you do the world a favor and stop producing radioactive orange sludge.

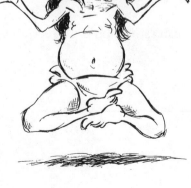

I Help...
Women Meet Men

If You're Desperate To Meet Men Just Go Speeding. This tip from my younger sister. A little something for the women who've stuck with this writing.

I Seek My Soulmate By All Means At My Disposal

In this fast paced, technological world we live in there is rarely time to seek out that special life partner. How often have you wished for a dating service that would help you meet people you're compatible with, find attractive and have a spiritual belief structure similar to yours? Your prayers have been answered. Spiritual Connections is here.

The process is easy. Simply call us for a survey sheet, fill it out and return it with $20.00. Once we have it our crack staff of professional dating spiritualists will begin to pray for you to find that special some-one. Does this work, you ask? It certainly can't hurt.

I Warn People Offended...
By Anti-Feminist Humor

If you are offended by anti–feminist humor, of which much has crept into this book of affirmations, then we ask you to avoid the next one. It contains many elements of a jibe and will surely offend anyone who takes feminism seriously. You have been warned.

The preceding warning has been offered by "We're not all bad." A bunch of guys who really are trying to figure out how to relate to angry empowered feminists. You can call us toll free at 1–800–UKICKME with any complaints you may have. Please, we really want to understand where you're coming from. Just give us a chance to prove we're not like all the other guys you've met. PLEASE.

I Watch Star Trek...
Feminists In Space

Gene Roddenbery's vision of the future included a ship of women devoted to furthering the rights of women in the universe. In this startling new series Marilyn French stars as Captain Bly of the ship NCC – PC. Her crew includes a Klingon first officer with sexual orientation confusion, a trans-sexual Feringi and a transvestite oriental Vulcan. Together they form the nucleus of the most politically correct ship in Star Fleet.

The two hour premiere has as special guest star Andrea Dwarkin. Andrea acci-dentally becomes a black hole after failing at Jenny Craig for the fifth time and gain-ing infinite mass. The resulting blow to the space time continuum sends her forward in time and space where she is picked up by Captain Bly and the PC, after dieting down to finite mass. Andrea returns to her work of legislating men guilty of rape in all instances of sexual intercourse because women have been victimized for so long that they can't make a choice like that for themselves. The whole show degenerates in a politically correct monologue for the next ninety minutes.

Hey wait, this is just like *Star Trek : Voyager*. What gives? Who'd want to watch Voyager anyway? Who really wants to look at Captain Amway walking around with her arm akimbo the whole show? Give me Kirk, Spock, Scotty and Bones any day, at least those shows had plots. I hate what's happened to the Star Trek spin–offs.

I Conserve Water

A merica is overweight and it's costing us precious water. All those fat people who walk the streets are carrying a large supply of water in their bodies and it's time we reclaimed it. The statistics are staggering.

Let's say the average American is 20 pounds overweight. With approximately 250 million of us in this country that amounts to 5 billion pounds that's serving no useful purpose. Now, since the body is 95% water, that comes to 4.75 billion pounds of water. With a gallon of water weighing seven pounds that translates into 678, 571, 428 gallons of water. How much more proof do you need? Conserve water, shoot a fat person.

I Am...
A Victim
In The Battle Of The PC

A battle is being waged between two groups, both PC. One is the left Politically Correct, the other is the right Patriotically Correct. Both are scary as hell. Let's compare the two

Politically Correct	*Patriotically Correct*
1. Believe the right is scum.	Believe the left is scum.
2. Believe the government can create equality and happiness.	Believe business can create equality and happiness.
3. Believe America was built by gays, by lesbians and albino cross–dressers.	Believe America was built by white Christian men only.
4. Love the environment	Hate the environment.
5. Shame based.	Shame based.
6. Have ugly spokespeople.	Have ugly spokespeople in nice clothes.
7. Blame right for all problems.	Blame left for all problems.
8. Should lighten up.	Should wake up.

I Summarize...
The Mists Of Avalon

Arthur...

I fucked my sister. Oopps. Don't cry Gwenhwyfar, here I'll renounce all that I've vowed. It's okay that you're a barren bitch. Here sleep with Lancelot and me. I have a son by my sister. How come everyone is trying to kill me? I'm such a good Christian. Patricide sucks.

Gwenhwyfar...

I don't like pagans. I'm a pristine Christian woman who want's to fuck my husband's best friend. Three is better than two. I'm barren, Arthur must have sinned. He did what with Morgaine? Bad pagans. I'm so pretty. I'm not pretty. I wish I were like Morgause so I'll condemn her actions. I want Lancelot. I have Lancelot. Now that I have Lancelot I'll have him take me to a convent. At least I'll be indoors.

Morgaine...

I'm one of the fairy folk. I have to take care of my brother. I'm a priestess. Isn't the goddess wonderful. I fucked my brother. Oopps. Viviane is a bitch. I have abandoned Avalon. Camelot sucks. I can't stand to see Lancelot and Gwenhwyfar being foolish, I'll set up Lancelot to sleep with another woman and get caught. It's the will of the Goddess. North Wales sucks except for Accolon. I want to die. I'm Lady of the Lake. Arthur was killed by his son. The Goddess won in the end.

I Have Found The World's Best Experiential Training

We here at MindFuck Inc. have devised the ultimate experiential training and are proud to finally present it to you, the discerning public. Over the past few years we have carefully attended the best the seminars and synthesized the diverse teachings into an elegant and effective experience sure to open you to yourself in ways undreamed of.

Our approach is simple. We shame you into performing well. "Had a rough childhood? So what! Other people have had worse and done very well with their lives. Quit your bellyaching and get back to work." That's just a sample of what you'll receive at our training.

Imagine 200 people chanting wimp at you as you explain why you're scared of something. It's an incredible mechanism. We take your worst fears, actualize them and make you deal with them; all the while not being supported or loved. Imagine how easy the real world will seem compared to how horribly we will treat you.

So open up your checking accounts, prepare to hand over your free will and get your ass into our training.

Respectfully,

MindFuck Inc.

I Win

The competition was intense. As we rounded the final curve I got a burst of speed and shot past Kaetlin. Just before making her move a car blocked the path. I was on the other side and had a free and clear path to the front door of the house. On my next turn I rolled a four, two more than I needed, and I jumped my piece to the door step; winning the game.

It was a tough, grueling victory. The type of victory that only those who compete against four year olds in the game of *101 Dalmatians* can understand. The bitterness, the hatred and the rivalry were all there as we battled to be the one to put the Dalmatian cut–outs into their respective slots. How I laughed and danced when her path was blocked by that car. And then I was able to taunt her after I had won, yes won, the game. Victory is never sweeter than when achieved over a pre–schooler.

Musician...
Know What Love Is

J. Geils	It stinks.
Nazareth	It hurts.
Bette Midler	It's a gift.
Dire Strait	It's related to express ways.
Beatles	It's all you need
Big Head Todd And The Monsters	It's bittersweet.
Golden Earring	It's radar.
Ricki Lee Jones	Chuck E.'s in it.

So from all these diverse sources I now see what love can be.

It can be a beating delivered by a smelly police officer to a guy named Chuck E. after Chuck is caught by a radar speed trap on the express way.

It can be a gift of bittersweets given along with a note saying it's all you need.

I Am Unwilling
To Give Blowjobs

I'm thinking about trying to break into show business, or should I say "bidness", and I'm concerned. Am I going to severely limit my career options by not being willing to give blowjobs? Not that I couldn't learn. I bet I could give a really good blowjob if I put my mind to it. It's just that my current doesn't run AC/DC.

I Wish Happy Holidays

B y this I mean "Merry Christmas and a Happy New Year." None of this politically correct manure. It doesn't mean "Merry Christmas or, if you're Jewish, Happy Chanukah (however the hell it's spelled), or, if you're an African American, Joyous Kwanza or, if you're an agnostic, Merry Whatever You Don't Believe In or, if you're an atheist, I'm sorry for pushing my religio–centric views on you."

If the phrase Merry Christmas offends you then learn to deal with it. And don't even get me started on how there is a move afoot to replace The Three Wise Men with The Culturally Diverse, Ethnically Balanced, and Sexually Confused Trio That Wasn't Any Wiser Than Any Other Randomly Chosen Group Of Three.

I'm Glad
My Sister Isn't Dating
An Ugly Guy

O ver the past weekend my younger sister, Beth, brought her new boyfriend by my older sister's house. The report from my older sister, Kathy. was "he's cute, but very quiet." My response, "I'm glad to hear Beth is dating someone cute."

I spoke with Beth later and told her of my happiness. "Hey Beth. I got the report from Kathy and I'm glad to hear you're dating someone cute."

"Yeah, he's pretty cute. But he's also very cool. Which is much more important."

"Beth, I've never known you to date someone who wasn't cute."

"Well no, but they were all cool. Besides, I think that people who are cool tend to be happy with themselves and that enhances their looks."

I about fall down laughing. She sounds like a Miss America contestant talking about how she wants a career in modeling, schooling and is ultimately going to be a brain surgeon who refurbishes children's hospitals in her spare time. "So if the Elephant Man were extremely cool you'd date him?" I ask laughing. I can hear her backpedaling.

I Drive A Chevy Because It's ... Like a rock.

Like a large mass of stone forming a hill, cliff, promontory or the like.

Like mineral matter of variable composition, consolidated or unconsolidated, assembled in masses or considerable quantities in nature, as by the action of heat or water.

Like a stone in the mass.

Like a stone of any size.

Like something resembling a rock.

Like a stupid metaphor.

I Think...
Guys Who Play Video Games
Are Punks

It always amazes me when I see some geek playing a video game who walks away strutting after finishing the game or finishing off a human challenger. Not that they actually fight. No, not that. They move a joystick around and press buttons. With certain combinations they make their "character" do flips, kicks, secret moves and taunts. All the while they stand staring at a television screen thinking they know how to fight.

After teaching martial arts for over a decade, two things are readily apparent. One is that it is very difficult to pull someone's spine out. A slight error results in picking their nose. Two is that beginners don't know their right from their left. The phrase of choice for the errant beginner is "Your other right."

So for all you video addicted geeks, of which I am one, please remember that just because you know how to play Scorpion, Smoke, Guile, E. Honda, Shun and Jackie to the end of their respective games it doesn't mean you know how to actually fight. I dare say you'd run away screaming if you were ever confronted by any of the characters you are so fond of beating up. That is of course if they didn't drop a hand grenade down your throat first.

I...

Have A Marketing Idea

Tattoo coporate insignias on the bodies of athletes. If it's good enough for funny cars it's good enough for Michael Jordan.

I Am...
Pessimistic

Did you know that within ten years we'll have lost enough bio–mass that the Earth will no longer be able to support life? Did you know that Canadian cod fishing is nearly destroyed? They might have overfished them so much that cod will become extinct. Isn't that horrible. Did you know that world wide frog populations have been decreasing for the past ten years? Do you know what all this means? Life as we know it on this planet is over.

Did you know that consumers spent less this Christmas than expected? Do you know what this means? It means that American consumers have lost their faith in the future. This means that there is going to be a dramatic downturn in investment which is going to cause the stockmarket to bottom out. Companies are going to fold. There's going to be massive unemployment. The Great Depression is going to look like a mild recession in comparison. Life as we know on this planet is over.

We're going to lose the next election. They are going to be in control. Life as we know it on this planet is over.

I Want...
To Be Elected

My campaign is based on three simple principles; happiness, wealth and youthful immortality. If elected I first will work to pass legislation making everyone happy. As an added incentive it will be a felony to be unhappy, which should put the vast majority of radical feminists into federal prison. Where they really belong.

The second piece of legislation addresses wealth. I want every happy American to be wealthy. My dream is that the government will give every American one million dollars. I will work to make this dream a reality.

Finally, all happy, wealthy Americans deserve immortality. I promise to get legislation passed declaring every American youthfully immortal. The aging process will be outlawed and anyone caught aging will have to share a cell with a radical feminist until they decide to stop aging.

Please remember on election day that a vote for me is a vote for happiness, wealth and youthful immortality.

I Believe...
The World Bank
Has The World's Interests
At Heart

We at the World Bank are distressed by the concern people have over the extinction of certain animals. From a strictly economic perspective, animals are a liability. They take up valuable real estate, produce nothing but themselves and occasionally kill productive employees. Why animals even get in the way of us properly polluting most third world countries.

Who really misses the Passenger Pigeon? We here at the World Bank can't remember the last person who said, "Gee, I wonder what the ol' Passenger Pigeons would be doing if they were alive today." Out of sight, out of mind. The same will happen with other species. In a hundred years who's going to care about eagles, whales and dolphins? No one. As long as we placate the masses with domesticated, productive creatures, like the cow, they should be happy.

Our recommendation is to begin a strong advertising campaign showing how much better the world would be if the Saran Ghetti was an industrial complex, the rain forest a chemical factory and of, course, the oceans a giant garbage dump.

I Fear...
The Circumvention
Of Darwin

The world is getting safer. At least the United States is getting safer. Okay, at least United States' playgrounds are getting safer. At the very least there are more law suits against playground equipment manufacturers because children have been hurt on "unsafe" equipment. There is a cry for completely safe playground equipment being championed by today's parents. I totally disagree.

I am frightened at this prospect. The world is in pretty rough shape now and we've had thousands of years of evolution leaving us with the best and the brightest our gene pool has to offer. Imagine, if you can, how badly someone who doesn't know how to use a slide is going to fuck up the environment. For the future of the world I urge you to get rid of your car seats, bike helmets and make sure you have good, old fashioned, unsafe playground equipment for your children to play on. We can not have a bright future with Darwinism being circumvented.

I Hate Buttons
and Bumper Stickers

I often wonder about people who have lots of buttons and/or bumper stickers. Are they proudly reminding themselves of their views on important topics such as abortion, politics and whirled peas or are they insecure wimps who need props to define who they are? I am leaning towards the latter.

Does the person who wears a button that "makes a statement" really believe anyone else is going to change their opinion? Perhaps they believe someone driving behind them will have an epiphany because their bumper sticker. "Gosh, I've been wrong about this whole abortion thing. That bumper sticker really opened my eyes." This is not going to happen.

For all you people who will have your gun pried from your cold dead hand or voted for Clinton/Gore in 1996 or think mean people suck or visualize Slim Pickins or are pro–choice or pro–life or advertise any of your views with bumper stickers or buttons, get a clue. The only person you're impressing or influencing is yourself.

I Have Questions...
For Western Medicine

Do brain storms hurt?

Why do they call it a heart attack when it's actually a heart retreat?

If I have a stroke while golfing do I have to add or subtract it from my score?

If donating organs is so noble, why don't hospitals and doctors donate their resources for the transplants?

I Hold...
Spirit Gently

Y ou better not mess up that ceremony. Did you say your
prayers correctly? Are you absolutely certain that mantra
is right? Pitch perfect when you say "Om?"

I'd hate for you to do anything wrong because if you do not
do all these things absolutely right you are going to break Spirit.
If your altar is not immaculate, Spirit will leave your life. If you
break someone else's toys, Spirit will send a messenger to teach
you a lesson. Actually, Spirit is just looking for an excuse to
dump your sorry ass of a soul in the ol' Cosmic Garbage
Disposal. So you better be careful. You better not make any
mistakes. Or "WHAM!" Spirit's going to slam you upside the
head when you least expect it. Just like my older brother did to
me when I was growing up.

I'd Rather Eat Oreos...
Than Animal Crackers

With the holiday season approaching we, the members of PETAC – People for the Ethical Treatment of Animal Crackers, wish to remind the population of the cruelty of eating animal crackers. From adults who slowly bite the limbs off of the crackers to the small children who wantonly waste precious crackers there is a blantant disregard for the sanctity of animal crackers. And what about the message eating animal crackers sends to people? Are we not symbolically eating meat? It is simply a carnivores Eucharist. What's next? Blood flavored High–C? We must, at the very least, begin eating our animal crackers in a humane way. Please, please, please bite off the heads of your animal crackers first. Spare these poor, defenseless, cookies the agony and terror of being eaten alive. Thank you for empathyisizing with our baked friends.

Today...
I Will Sleep
When I Am Tired

Except if you're operating heavy machinery, that would be a bad idea.

Too often we don't listen to our bodies when we're tired. Sleepiness rolls over us like a gentle wave and we push it back with the barricade of caffeine. Depriving ourselves of our necessary sleep is a fool hardy thing. I believe that there are "batteries" that get recharged when we sleep. If those batteries aren't properly charged there are several effects. In the short term, I think sleep creeps up on us and suddenly we sleep for fifteen instead of six hours. For chronic sleep deprivation I believe the stress induced reduces the life span. And who knows where that can lead.

I encourage you to listen to your body. When you're tired, instead of slamming that two liter bottle of Mountain Dew, get some rest. I'd give you a meditation, but I'm afraid writing one would put me to sleep. I'm really tired right now, but I want to get this affirmation done.

Take it from me, Today I Will Sleep When I Am Tired!

I Ignore My Body

I'm tired. My feet hurt. The arrow in my arm is very painful.

How many times have we used excuses like these to avoid getting things done? And where do all these excuses stem from? The body. The truth is the body just gets in the way most of the time. How many times have pain and tiredness in the body worked against you? I'll bet a lot. Here's my solution; I ignore my body.

It has worked wonders for me. One time I ran a marathon and at about the halfway point I felt a stinging pain in my calf. If I had listened to my body I would have quit the marathon. But I kept on running, ignoring the pain as it grew into a excruciating tearing running the length of my left leg. Even though I collapsed in agony at the finish line I finished the race! They wheeled me off to the ambulance with my participants medal pinned to my chest. It was one of my proudest moments. Of course I walk with a limp today and I lost the medal during my last move. But it was all worth it for that gold–plated, quarter–sized medal that was cradled perfectly by one of my Elvis statuettes. So you see, if you ignore your body you to can win cheap trinkets and never run again.

Ignore your body, it's worth it.

I Follow My Dreams

In this hectic, technological world that we live in sometimes it is easy to lose sight of our dreams. The rush to promote a career, buy a house, find the latest ceramic Elvis statuette and simply pay the bills can cloud over the dreams with a layer of really gunky gunk.

You know, the type of gunk that sticks to everything. It's usually black and you've got to scrub your hands really hard in order to remove it. And even once it's removed you can still feel it. And for some reason there is a dream gunk–like substance. That is the gunk you have to look out for if you're going to follow your dreams.

Of course I mean follow your good dreams. If I had meant that you should follow your nightmares I would have made that the affirmation. Perhaps nightmares are the accumulation of gunk which is then projected into a dream. So by all means don't pursue those kinds of dreams, that would be pretty stupid. Although Steven King has made a living out of writing about his gunk.

Okay, okay. If you're going to pursue your dreams, even the gunky ones, make sure you do it in a creative, non–destructive manner. Look to your dreams for guidance and assistance. Take small steps, but take at least a small step every day. With this in mind you should be able to find your way to the happiness your dreams bring to you, unless of course you pursue your nightmares. In that case you'll probably create a living hell for yourself. But if that's what you want, I support you one–hundred percent.

I See My Generation Clearly

I love how my generation has been defined. We are
Generation X; a bunch of slacker losers who's only contri-
bution to society has been cool Mountain Dew commercials.
Our icons are legendary. There's Spuds McKenzie, the original
party animal. Nothing sums our generation up more than Spuds,
a female posing as a male. There's a lot of that going around (to
be fair, there are a lot of men posing as women too). And a large
portion of my generation has grown so confused they've given
up and are now trying to look neutral, although that trend may
be a clever marketing ploy by Calvin Klein.

We pierce our body parts multiple times. We want our MTV.
We are directionless. We wear a lot of black and think it would
be cool to be a vampire. Some of us are Republicans. Some of
us are Democrats. There is no doubt about it, we are completely
messed up. Almost as messed up as every other generation.
Thank God Flappers haven't come back into style. Then again,
who really knows how Calvin Klein is going to market their
next perfume.

I Want To Help...
Illiterate People

I am deeply disturbed by the plight of the illiterate. What would it be like to go through life without being able to read? Why, you would not even be able to enjoy this wonderful and insightful book. And it saddens me that no illiterate person will ever be able to enjoy my book. I am also deeply saddened and concerned by the loss of sales. There are millions of potential buyers out there for my writing and without your help they may never know the humor to be found in this book. So go. Go and find an illiterate person. Buy them a copy of my book, *This Book Won't Help You*, and help them learn to read. You'll be doing them, and me, a big favor.

Today...
I Will Glance

Single Scoping Glance...

The Single Scoping Glance (SSG) is usually delivered when a brief look is desired. The eyes flick to the left or right and then back to center. The eyes remain in motion during the whole glance. This appears to be more reflex than anything else in most people. The appearance of multiple SSGs is an indication of physical attraction or curiosity, i.e. trying to check out someone's disability without being too obvious.

I'm Busted...

The I'm Busted maneuver is usually performed by women who glance at men and accidentally make eye contact, or know that they've been seen looking. Shame on them. To make up for their blatant hussiness said woman will quickly look at a point four feet in front of her toes. This is usually coupled with trying to look meek, humble and demure.

Depending on the guy there are a variety of responses. Some simply approach the woman and begin a conversation. On the opposite end of the spectrum the suave meister will turn beet red and run the opposite direction.

Forty–five degree angle glance...

I'm very grateful to my friend Cara for sharing this, to my knowledge, exclusive glancing style of women. It is usually executed after a SSG. If the attraction is there but a better, confirming, method is needed the woman will turn her head so that her line of sight is forty–five degrees off the target. She can then scope with anonymity. Very clever, I was impressed.

I Achieve...
The Eleventh Insight

James Redfield needs deodorant. How did I get this insight? Did I read it in a book? Did someone tell me? Was it on television? No. I intuited it. I looked inside, I introspected. The insight came from inner sight. After obtaining this insight I looked for a more logical answer, the tangible information that can be part of a deductive process. What I concluded surprised me.

James Redfield, author of the best selling *The Celestine Prophecy*, has no clue what an insight is. Throughout his writing he makes the error of presenting exposition, narrative and reading as equivalents to insight. I have concluded since he doesn't know what an insight is and wrote a book that stinks, illustrating his ignorance, he must also stink. It is well known that bad smelling literature is created by people who smell bad, except me.

James, if you're reading, you owe me. From your own book, "The manuscript says our incomes will remain stable because of people who are giving us money for the insights we provide." Cough up. I want at least fifteen dollars for my insight into your body odor problem. That'll pay for your stupid book.

To Love My Lover

I discovered you on a night long ago

A magical mystery to behold

I grasped you reflexively

Without great passivity

Now time has flown by

And it seems you are always on my arm

Always helping me to avoid harm

Diversely living life boldly

I dare say I hold you as holy

You are my teacher and my student

A wise mentor who is always prudent

Grant one request to your greatest fan

Please reconcile with my other hand